*Robert H. Culpepper*

Dover Memorial Library
Gardner-Webb University
P.O. Box 836
Boiling Springs, N.C. 28017

# THE EVOLUTION OF CHRISTOLOGY

# THOR HALL

# THE
# EVOLUTION
# OF
# CHRISTOLOGY

ABINGDON
Nashville

BT
202
.H244
1982

# THE EVOLUTION OF CHRISTOLOGY

*Copyright © 1982 by Abingdon*

All rights reserved.
No part of this book may be reproduced in any manner
whatsoever without written permission of the publisher
except brief quotations embodied in critical articles
or reviews. For information address Abingdon,
Nashville, Tennessee

**Library of Congress Cataloging in Publication Data**

HALL, THOR, 1927—
    The evolution of Christology.

    1. Jesus Christ—Person and offices—Addresses, essays, lectures. I. Title.
BT202.H25        232        81-14838        AACR2

**ISBN 0-687-12190-6**

Scripture quotations unless otherwise noted are from the Revised Standard Version of the Bible, copyrighted 1946, 1952, 1971, © 1973, by the Division of Christian Education of the National Council of the Churches of Christ in the U.S.A., and used by permission.

Quotations noted TEV are from the Bible in Today's English Version. Copyright © American Bible Society 1966, 1971, 1976.

The poem on page 109 is from Alice Meynell, *The Poems of Alice Meynell.* Wilfred Meynell, Editor. Copyright 1923 by Wilfred Meynell; copyright renewed. Reprinted with the permission of Charles Scribner's Sons.

MANUFACTURED BY THE PARTHENON PRESS
NASHVILLE, TENNESSEE, UNITED STATES OF AMERICA

In memory of

My Mother

MARGIT ELVIRA HALL
nee Petersen

1900-1975


*She taught me that first simple
song about Jesus*

# CONTENTS

# PREFACE

This little book is the result of the combination of several interests that have been mine for a number of years, but which I have not heretofore been able to bring together in direct interaction, namely, biblical theology, doctrinal or historical theology, and systematic or constructive theology.

That these dimensions of theology need to be combined seems clear—any one of these disciplines separated from the others will undoubtedly show the effects of such isolation. That they can now be combined, in my case, is due primarily to the discovery—which I can only claim to be new for me—that all theology deserving of this name, whether biblical, historical, or contemporary, participates in a single spiritual-intellectual dynamic: an evolutionary process of faith and thought that takes place in the context of continuing change—changing situations, changing religious awareness, changing thought-forms, changing language.

Theology has often denied its relativity to change—or, if it has acknowledged it, considered it only as affecting the *logy*, not the *theo*, of theology. Thought and language may have been considered contextual-situational, and therefore changing, but not the faith, not the truth, not the message of Christianity. These elements are absolute, given, permanent. The *form* of theology may change, but not the *content*; the *terminology* may vary, but not the *meaning*; *reason* is relative, but not *revelation*; *fides quae* (that which faith believes) may change, but not *fides qua* (faith itself).

Such denial of relativity or separation of absolute and relative elements in theology was always suspect from any historical-empirical

9

or phenomenological point of view. What makes it virtually impossible for those of us who do theology today to continue this line of thought is quite simply the observation that faith is as much an aspect of human perception as is thought, and meaning as clearly empirical as language. Even revelation, when it occurs, occurs to human reason. Man does not believe with one faculty and think with another; he does not perceive meaning on one channel and express it on another. Both the *theos* and the *logos* of theology are anchored in human awareness and experience; both, moreover, are related—relative—to history, to situation and context, and therefore subject to change.

This observation, not in itself particularly dramatic or radical, takes on deeper meaning when combined with the insight that Christian faith and thought, both, have in fact been subject to change and development through history—and that, not only *after* the formative period, as evidence of a deterioration of theology and an increasing heteronomy (to use Tillich's terminology) of Christian faith and thought. This spiritual-intellectual process was already at work among the early fathers of the church and in the apostolic community—it was in fact the process through which Christian faith and thought were first formed. When one realizes this, and discovers evidence within the New Testament itself of a series of radical breakthroughs to new levels of faith and thought, the effect will become evident in the way one relates to all theology, past and present. One relates to the theologies of the past in entirely new ways, and one enters into the theological tasks of the present with altogether different attitudes. Specifically, one becomes more deeply involved in the dynamic that informed the theological developments in the past, and at the same time more genuinely free to enter into the theological processes that represent the growing edge of things in the present.

I must pause for a moment to give credit to three scholars whose books have been the midwives of my discovery, namely, Norman Perrin, G.W.H. Lampe, and Hans Küng. Norman Perrin's *The New Testament: An Introduction* (Harcourt Brace, 1974) takes a historical-evolutionary view of New Testament theology and convinces us not only that there are several different theological perspectives identifiable within the New Testament writings, but also that these perspectives represent successive and evolving stages of Christian faith and thought. Perrin argues that since the church in determining the New Testament canon included writings representative of each of these stages of development, the entire process from beginning to end is of importance to the understanding of the Christian message. Lampe's book *God as Spirit* (Clarendon Press, 1977) examines some of the earliest doctrinal developments in the church in the light of New Testament spirituality and spirit symbolism, and argues that the later trinitarian "hypostatization" of God's being and action in the world is more problematic and less useful as model for theology than the biblical concept of "inspiration." Lampe shows that inspiration is a continuing event and that the process of interpreting and reinterpreting God's presence and work in the world never comes to an end—it is possible, in fact, to move forward, to modify and even abandon earlier interpretations, in the light of the continuing guidance of the spirit of God, the Christ-spirit still at work among us. This is also what Hans Küng does. His book *On Being a Christian* (Doubleday, 1976) is precisely such a reinterpretation of the faith, partly with reference to the modern religious situation, where Christianity is confronted with a wide variety of ideologies and competing religious commitments, partly with reference to pre-dogmatic New Testament Christianity, which Küng takes to be the roots of the Christian faith tradition. In the process, Küng is quite critical of ancient church dogmas, which he describes as "late developments," flawed by reliance on Greek metaphysical concepts, since outdated, and declares as his own purpose "to defend, to justify and to clarify Christian faith, to face up to its naked challenge, when the cushioning upholstery of museum-piece dogmatics has been stripped aside" (remarks made before the Overseas Club, New York, November 8, 1976). The reader will hear echoes of Perrin's, Lampe's, and Küng's views at several points in the text that follows.

The focal point of these chapters is "Christology," that kind of theology—biblical, doctrinal, constructive—which centers on Christ. The reason for this orientation is explained at some length in chapter 1, entitled "The Scope and Focus of Christian Faith." Here I would simply point out that Christology in this book is not considered an *aspect* of theology or a *part* of the larger system of Christian doctrine—a *fragment of Christian* theology. Rather, I take Christology to be a definite *form* of theology, a distinct *way to do* theology—an approach to *all* theology. In my opinion, all Christian theology is Christocentric theology. It is precisely the christological perspective on theology that characterizes the Christian theologian and sets him apart from all other theologians.

This book, then, is really about Christian theology—Christocentric theology. It takes a developmental view of this theology, looking particularly at the dynamics of faith and thought in which this theology first manifested itself, in its original form or forms, in the New Testament. It then goes on to affirm that, as participants in the same theological dynamic, Christian theologians today must do for our time what New Testament Christians did for theirs, namely, allow our Christology to evolve and expand in interaction with situational changes, religious sensibilities, and intellectual advancements that are contextual to the Christian community today. My aim is twofold: to involve the reader deeply in the process of christological faith and thought that is evident in the New Testament and to inspire the contemporary Christian to enter freely and responsibly into the same sort of process in the present situation. Chapters 2 through 5 deal with four stages of development in New Testament christological reflection; chapters 6 and 7 deal with the christological task of the church in the space age.

Parts of this book have already been tested in various contexts. Chapter 3 is in large part lifted from my article "Let Religion Be Religious," published in *Interpretation*, April 1969. Chapter 7 was first read before the Section on Philosophy of Religion and Theology of the Southeastern Region of the American Academy of Religion in March 1979. Chapters 2 through 5 were given as lectures at the Georgia Area United Methodist Pastors' School in July 1978, and again—with the addition of chapters 1 and 6—as the Voigt Lectures sponsored by the Southern Illinois Conference of the United Methodist Church at McKendree College, Lebanon, Illinois, in

## PREFACE

January 1979. Portions of the book were also read at the Preachers' Collegium at the University of Tennessee at Chattanooga in May 1979 and at the South Carolina United Methodist Pastors' School in September 1979. In addition, several personal friends, lay and clergy, have read the manuscript.

In all these contexts I have been gratified by the response, and have reaped great benefit from sound and helpful criticism. I have also benefited from editorial comments by the publisher's readers and staff. This does not mean, however, that the book is now without edges or that it has been proven "safe"—it carries no official imprimatur. I anticipate further criticism and much discussion.

Personal appreciation must be expressed to a number of people who have helped me in this project—from those who invited me to give these lectures and thus imposed an unbending deadline, to the publisher who saw meaning in what was written and gave opportunity for last-minute revisions. My secretary, Mrs. Faye Hubbard, and our assistant, Ms. Sharon Rose, showed great patience as usual in typing and retyping the manuscript. My son Jan is credited with having suggested a title which after several detours reappeared as the publisher's choice as well, and my wife with numerous instances of refinement of meaning and clarification of language, throughout. I am grateful, as ever.

*T.H.*

## CHAPTER 1

The Scope and Focus
of Christian Faith

If we should ask one another, those of us who share the Christian faith, what Christianity is all about—how we describe the content and character of this faith—most of us would probably fall back on the general definitions with which we grew up, statements which have come down to us from generations past and now serve in the way of catechetical capsules among us, such as, "Christian faith is faith in Christ," "Christianity is defined by the Word of God."

These are formulations most of us are comfortable with, both clergy and laity. They function effectively in theological shorthand. They are seldom analyzed, never questioned. They are so basic, so fundamental, that any and all Christians are expected to agree. We use them interchangeably. We consider them clear until we realize that the definition of Christianity presents us with a troublesome dilemma.

We are faced, on the one hand, with *the particularity, the uniqueness, the central point of Christian faith,* and on the other with *the generality, the universality, the inclusiveness of the Christian message.* What Christianity is all about cannot be defined simply by reference to the essence and core of Christian faith—its "focus"; Christianity must also be defined in terms of the expanse and circumference of its content—its "scope." But this is precisely where the dilemma lies: A definition which is concerned with the broad scope of the Christian message—the Word of God in all its dimensions—is not immediately useful in identifying the essential character of Christian faith; and a definition which is concerned with the character and focal point of Christian faith—its center and core,

Christ—is not immediately capable of incorporating the wider expanse of the Christian message.

Let me illustrate the problem autobiographically.

I remember, at my ordination, when the bishop, the district superintendent, and several sponsors all laid their hands on my head and the words of ritual were pronounced: "Take thou authority . . . to preach the Word of God," how strong and clear I thought those words were. It was as though everything behind me, all that was within me, and everything ahead of me came together in a single point—the task, the responsibility, and the privilege of being a minister of the Word. It all seemed so simple and straightforward at that point.

I came out of a tradition where the Bible, the whole Bible, was believed and confessed to be the revealed Word of God. So, as my right hand rested on an open Bible and the bishop pronounced the formula, "Take thou authority . . . to preach the Word of God," I knew what that meant: As a Christian minister I was to preach the Bible, the message of the Bible, the whole Bible. That's where the Word of God was set forth.

I soon learned, however, that preaching the Word—or rather, determining what Word to preach—is not all that simple. The Bible itself is not that simple. The Word of God is not just one word. The message of the Bible is not just one message.

I had, of course, studied theology. I had been exposed to historical-critical biblical scholarship, to the principles of hermeneutics and the methods of exegesis. I had delved deeply into the history of Christian thought and had a fair comprehension of the variations of interpretation and the differences among traditions. That was not what caused me problems. Knowledge was not what made my preaching uncertain.

It was the Bible itself. There is an Old Testament and a New Testament in it—an old covenant and a new. There is law and there is gospel; commandments and promises; judgment and grace; works and faith. There is the religion of Moses; the cult of the temple; the proclamations of the prophets—prophets of doom and prophets of salvation. And there is the message of John the Baptist; the teachings of Jesus; the kerygma of the apostles—apostles to the Jews and apostles to the Gentiles. The biblical message is a multitude of messages.

Which should I preach?

My tradition gave me little guidance. As a "free church," the Methodist Church in Norway had discarded all lectionaries and authoritative expositions. Texts should be chosen by the inspiration of the Holy Spirit, and the individual preacher—under the guidance of the Spirit—was to be his own authority as to the truth. I was to preach the Word as it was revealed to me.

So, while I started out in my ministry with the standpoint of a biblical fundamentalist—committed to the Bible, the whole Bible, and nothing but the Bible, as the Word of God—I soon developed the mind-set of an individualist, preaching only that which in my own subjective judgment had the ring of truth to it. I took an idealistic, even enthusiastic stance: The Word of God for any occasion was what God, through the Holy Spirit, had given me to say.

At my ordination, as the leaders of the church laid hands on me, the Bible on which my hand rested was opened to the Book of Job. I caught a glimpse of a passage, which I later went back to again and again in the years that followed. It was the opening part of the speech by Elihu, the angry young man who broke into the dialogue between Job and his "friends" with the following statement:

"I am young in years,
    and you are aged;
therefore I was timid and afraid
    to declare my opinion to you.
I said, 'Let days speak,
    and many years teach wisdom.'
But it is the spirit in a man,
    the breath of the Almighty, that makes him understand.
It is not the old that are wise,
    nor the aged that understand what is right.
Therefore I say, 'Listen to me;
    let me also declare my opinion.' " (Job 32:6-10)

17

This passage became something of a motto for me in those early years. It bolstered my courage; it shored up my independence. *My* word was also a word of God.

At this point I must confess one other thing about my early preaching ministry, the fact that my preaching, focused on declaring *my* opinion—the Word of God as *I* saw it—neither came to have the full scope of the biblical revelation nor the clear focus of Christian truth. This, of course, is hindsight, though not altogether so.

I found, in those early years as a preacher, that what I was inspired to say on any given occasion was directed more to my subjective perception of things—my own preoccupation at that moment—than to the larger perspectives, the deeper dimensions, the complete structure of the biblical message. In fact, I preached only those parts of the Bible which I happened to be interested in—or inspired by—at the time, namely, those parts which I thought had particular relevance to the contemporary situation or to the needs of the people in the pew. That left out a lot, altogether. Instead of being a servant of the Word, I was operating as its master.

Moreover, I found that my subjective perception changed from time to time—my focus shifted, often from week to week—wavering between different, even contrasting, emphases in the biblical revelation. At times I was preoccupied with grace; at other times by law. Sometimes I preached faith, faith *alone*, apart from works; sometimes I preached works as the only validation of faith. One Sunday I would sound like Moses; the next like Jeremiah; the third like John the Baptist; the fourth like Paul; and the fifth like James. What I said in one sermon had little to do with what I had said in the last one, or what I would say in the next one.

I was also, of course, concerned with the effect of my preaching—the response of the people. I began to suspect, in fact, that I was neither the servant of the Word, nor entirely its master, but rather a slave to the congregation.

It was not only that I wanted to build my reputation as a preacher; I wanted to increase numbers, have people respond positively—"enjoy" my sermons, as they say. So I was always on the lookout for that which was "popular." This did not mean, at all times, that I tried to do the extraordinary. Most of the time it brought me back to the very ordinary—what people expected, what they were comfortable with.

Let me tell you of the low point in this process. It came one Sunday, in a little Methodist church in Norway, where I muddled through the early stages of my ministry. Among the members of the church was a leading businessman in town, important in politics, in the community, and in the church, both locally and nationally. He was a licensed local preacher, a delegate to annual conference, a member of the executive council of the conference, a delegate to jurisdictional and general conferences. A powerful man. I had noticed over a period of time that his response to my sermons varied, and I thought I had discovered a system in it. Whenever I preached about God's love, God's unqualified goodness to men, God's promises and blessings, God's saving work in Christ, he seemed to respond beautifully; he was at ease in the pew, looked at me openly, nodding occasionally, and when he passed by at the door, I received a warm handshake and a friendly word. But whenever I preached about the demands of the gospel, the cost of discipleship, the cross we are to bear, the works we are called to do, his attitude seemed altogether different; he was impatient, bored, closed to his surroundings and shut up to my message, and when he passed me on the way out there was only a hurried "hello" or a half-extended hand.

Having broken his code, I worried about it. I found myself sliding away from the emphases which I thought he would not like, doing my best to make my sermons "acceptable in his sight"—that man's, that is. But I knew I was getting enslaved. Gone was my commitment to preach the Bible, the whole Bible. Gone was my conviction concerning the validity of the truth as revealed to me. Gone was the authority given me at my ordination, and my Elihu-inspired idealism and independence as well. I was trying to please him. But my conscience was bothered.

It went so far that for this particular Sunday I was prepared to preach two sermons—one if that man was present, another if he was not. Fortunately, he was not there, so I preached what I had hoped to be able to. But after that service, my personal and professional integrity in jeopardy, I made an appointment and went to see the man. I told him of my observations and my struggle and asked him point-blank what in his judgment was wrong with my preaching.

His response showed me clearer than I could have expected what a ridiculous enterprise it is to try to please a congregation or an individual member of it. He was embarrassed at the thought that his attitude and actions could have had such influence on the man in the pulpit. "How thoughtless and insensitive of me," he said. Then he explained. There was nothing at all wrong with my preaching; it was only that from time to time he suffered unbearably from a flare-up of his hemorrhoids. "When that happens," he said, "not even a Chrysostom can get through to me."

From that moment the two of us became fast friends—he knew my secret, and I knew his. More important yet, I was forever released from the bondage of gauging the validity of my preaching or the authenticity of my message by way of the response. That criterion is unreliable, to say the least.

But the issue remains—the question of the scope and focus of the Christian message. A preacher is always set on a sharp edge: on the one side the obligation to be inclusive in scope, to preach the whole counsel of God, God's Word in all its dimensions; on the other side the obligation to keep a sharp focus, to present the truth of Christ clearly and consistently and give the Christian faith integrity and authenticity. It is the same challenge every Christian believer faces: not to be so broad in scope as to lose a clear grasp of essential Christian faith, and not to be so narrow in focus as to ignore the larger dimensions of divine truth.

In the history of theology, the question of the scope and focus of Christian faith has given rise to considerable debate. There is in fact an entire spectrum of opinion on this question among theologians, past and present, from the broadest and most inclusive of views to the most pointed and particular.

Let me illustrate, by reference to the debate on the scope and focus of revelation.

The broadest and most inclusive view of revelation—and therefore of Christian faith—is *that of the universalist*. He sees God as revealing himself in all things, natural and historical, spiritual and material, sacred and secular. All science, all art, all religion are revelation. All meaning, all insight, all knowledge are revelation. All men, all cultures, all ages are recipients of revelation. No one is favored, no one left out. God makes his truth known universally, and God's truth is the same throughout.

The universalist view is a bold and attractive one, and has always had special attraction for those who think of God in a big way, especially for radical monotheists and unitarians who see God as one, as a single unity, and who take the entire world to be his domain. In this tradition, there is no limit to the scope of faith: God speaks everywhere; the believer must listen to everything. There is a problem, however, with focus. Revelation easily becomes so broad as to lose its contours; God's Word so general as to be shapeless. Christianity itself is swallowed up in world religion, and the Christian message is robbed of any separate identity.

A second, slightly narrower view of revelation is that which includes, yet separates between, a "general" and a "special" revelation. It is *the catholic*—though not specifically Roman Catholic—*view*, developed in the Middle Ages and set forth in the grand synthetic system of Thomas Aquinas, inspired not only by the biblical message, but by classical philosophy, especially Aristotle, as well. It sees God revealing his Word in a number of ways, in natural law as well as in divine law. God's will and wisdom can be comprehended both by reason and by faith. There is a "natural theology" and there is "revealed theology"; they are related much like two stories in a building, one accessible to every man, the other only to men of faith. "General revelation" is the light that shines in all men; "special revelation" is that light—the superior truth—that was manifest in Christ and set forth in Holy Scripture.

The catholic synthesis of nature and the supernatural, reason and revelation, has had and still has a wide following. It is a view that in some form carries attraction among orthodox or conservative theologians, who on its terms can continue to think of culture as dominated by christian revelation—Christendom—as well among liberal or progressive theologians, who, on the same assumption, proceed to construct a Christian apologetic along the lines of Tillich's method of correlation. This view appears to be both broad in scope and clear in focus; the Christian message is seen to have something to say about culture in general as well as of Christ, specifically. However, the matter is not so simple. The problem lies partly in the nature of the synthesis: Classical Christendom is clearly a form of Christian imperialism, and this mind-set is still present in contemporary correlation apologetics. The main difficulty with the correlation method, however, is its claim that reason and revelation stand in a relationship marked by both continuity and discontinuity. The believer must not only be able to operate on two levels—the level of reason and the level of revelation—he must also be able to determine where the one ends and the other begins. Here the lines tend to be blurred; the believer easily gets confused both about the scope and the focus of Christian faith.

A third major view of revelation is *that of the Biblicist.* It narrows revelation to that which is written in the Bible and denies both the existence of any general revelation and the possibility of any natural theology. God's Word is set forth in Holy Scripture, period. Reason cannot comprehend it; only faith, captured by the Word, can.

The Biblicist's viewpoint is also widely dispersed among us. It comes in several forms—from the fundamentalist view of literal inspiration and biblical inerrancy to the neo-orthodox view of divine self-proclamation and progressive revelation. In either form, the scope of faith is radically reduced; it is oriented to a text, based on the written Word—whether taken literally, as the fundamentalist does, or symbolically-kerygmatically, as the neo-orthodox does.

Having narrowed the scope of revelation, and thus of faith, one should think that the Biblicist had gained clarity of focus as well. But this is by no means the case. The Bible, as we have said before, contains many messages. The Word of God has many facets. The Book is many books. For the fundamentalist, of course, it is all equally normative. But this puts a great deal of pressure on him to demonstrate the unity and consistency of the Bible—which he does by way of non-historical exegesis and cross-reference. Neo-orthodox theologians try more sophisticated methods, allowing for a developing awareness of divine truth and accounting for any remaining contrasts by way of a unique dialectic of paradox. But the effect, in both cases, is vagueness; at times, as with the fundamentalist, inconsistency of emphasis—God's love and God's wrath, God's law and grace, accepted with equal finality and conviction—and at times, as with the neo-orthodox, mind-boggling complexity, making it a virtue *not* to understand, *not* to make sense. Thus the Biblicist believer has serious problems, both in regard to scope and in regard to focus.

A fourth view of revelation, designed to solve the problem the Biblicist has with focus, is narrower yet, namely, the *evangelical view*. Here revelation is limited to the gospel—though what the gospel is seen to be may vary somewhat among evangelicals. For some, like Marcion, the gospel is limited to the New Testament; only *it* contains a Christian message, while the Old Testament is a Jewish book, purely legalistic, no part of the gospel of grace at all. For others, like Luther, the gospel has to do with justification by faith or some other central doctrine, like blood atonement, which is then sought and lifted up, to the exclusion of everything else—Luther even went so far as to read certain books out of the Bible altogether because they were like mangers, "right strawy," he said, without the Christ. More recently, the evangelical view has crystalized itself in mottoes like "Good News," "God's Way of Salvation," "Four Spiritual Laws," and so forth, all attempts to capsule the essence of revelation, the Christian message, in a nutshell.

The strength of the evangelical view is its intention to focus on central Christian truths; its weakness is a radically restricted scope. Not only does a great deal of the biblical message fall out of the picture; the gospel itself is often restricted to those aspects of the faith that have to do with individual salvation. In the evangelical view, the question of scope is in fact reduced to the question of focus; all God says is contracted into a single, self-enclosed point. And the point is static. The message is given, once for all; God has already said all there is to say.

A fifth view of revelation to be included here is *the subjective-existentialist view*. Here revelation is not so much a historical event, manifest in a Word or a message out of the past, as it is a present, ongoing experience, realized in the life of the believer at the present.

The truth of Christianity is not so much "the truth once delivered to the saints"; it is the believer's own immediate awareness of truth—the Word of God as it confronts us now and evokes in us a conviction, a sense of meaning, a commitment to life in the light of that Word in the present.

The subjective view of revelation may, at times, have little or no connection with the scope and focus of historical Christian faith; if that happens, there is little reason to take this approach seriously as part of the Christian understanding of things at all. But subjective-existentialist approach is usually, at least as far as Christian existentialism is concerned, oriented to the personal appropriation of the message proclaimed—in the case of Christian existentialism, the existential meaning of the kerygma of the gospel. If this is the case, the existentialist view of revelation can potentially be seen to include both the broad scope of historical Christian faith and a clear focus on personal faith commitment.

It must be noted, however, that in actuality and practice the subjective-existentialist view does not always come off so clearly balanced. It happens, for example, when subjectivity or existential meaningfulness becomes not simply the focal point of an interpretive or communicative process, but a filter through which the Christian message itself is processed, that the existentialist focus is allowed to determine the scope of the Christian message itself. The theological method thus easily comes to dominate the content of the faith, and the result is both an irresponsible narrowing of scope and an unfortunate loss of focus.

A sixth and final view of revelation within the spectrum we are surveying here is one now usually described as *the ideological approach*. What characterizes ideology is the commitment to some "idea," some preconception which becomes normative both for the perception and the communication of the faith. Everything is interpreted in the light of this idea; everything is presented as a manifestation of it.

The ideological approach to the Christian message comes in many different forms; from one perspective a person might consider some of the views already presented as manifestations of ideology as well.

However, ideology is recognizable as such by the fact that it includes a definite element of manipulation. The ideologist does not stand humbly before the Christian message, simply observing and honestly presenting this message the way it is in itself; he puts his own slant on it, captures it within the categories of his own choice, and reshapes it to fit his own ideological image. Examples of such manipulations of Christianity are plentiful in the history of theology—from the Gnostics' formulation of a "higher wisdom" in the first and second centuries to Harnack's reinterpretation of the essence of Christianity in terms of "God, immortality, and the moral good" in the twentieth. Recently, the ideological approach to revelation has manifested itself in a number of new theologies—secular theology, with its emphasis on worldliness and common humanity, political theology, with its emphasis on liberation, and many more.

From the standpoint of the believer, the ideological stance provides perhaps the clearest focus of all. But it has a problem with scope. The perspective of the ideologist tends to be restricted to the exegesis of those parts of the Christian message which are in line with his own leading idea; at times, in fact, the ideologist tends to rework the Christian message by way of *eisegesis*—reading into the Bible the ideas he desires to draw from it. One tends therefore to be somewhat suspicious of this approach—that is, if he is not a part of it. If one is, then he accepts it uncritically. From a critical standpoint, the approach has obvious deficiencies, in regard to the focus as well as the scope of Christian faith.

Having surveyed the spectrum of answers, we find the question as troublesome as ever. The responsible Christian believer must be sure that his faith encompasses both the full scope of the Word of God and the particular focus of the gospel. He must align himself to the whole truth of God, yet retain a clear orientation to the Christian message; he must be responsive to the broad sweep of divine revelation and at the same time be committed to the ultimacy of the unique revelation in Christ. The question of the scope and focus of Christian faith is in actuality a whole series of questions rolled into one: What is the relationship between revealed truth and all other truth? Between special revelation and general revelation? Between formative revelation and ongoing revelation? What is the relationship between God's action in history and his work in nature? Between creation and redemption? Between salvation and consummation? What is the relationship between Christianity and the world's religions? Between the Old Testament and the New Testament? Between theism and Christology?

Such questions are serious. They cannot be answered by theological fiat—by declaring one side of the equation more important than the other and ignoring the rest. Neither can they be answered by way of paradox—by holding both sides in equal importance but not explaining how they can be held together. The only satisfactory answer is one that can satisfy fully the dual concern for inclusiveness in scope and particularly in focus—and that can be, at one and the same time, logically consistent and theologically competent.

Allow me to propose an outline of an answer by way of six propositions—a procedure which will serve at once to explain the standpoint I have chosen here and to introduce the perspectives that are applied in the following chapters. It will also bring to center stage the main theme of this book: Christology.

## Proposition 1: Christian faith is unapologetically Christocentric.

This speaks directly to the question of focus and defines the particularity of Christian faith as having to do with Christ. The point is elemental: Christianity is not Christian if it is not Christocentric. It is precisely the centrality of Christ that makes Christianity what it is. Christian faith is essentially faith in Christ.

We must note, however, that Christocentricity in focus does not mean that Christianity is restricted within any kind of Christomonism, or that Christology—or a kind of Jesusology—is all there is to the Christian message or to Christian faith. The Christocentricity that characterizes Christianity has to do with the *perspective*, not the purview, of Christian faith. The Christian believer does not simply look at Christ; he looks at all things in view of Christ. The role of Christology is not to circumscribe the content of Christian faith; rather, Christology determines the viewpoint from which the Christian considers all faith content.

## Proposition 2: Christocentricity is a form of theocentricity.

This affirms the continuity of Christian preaching with the whole of biblical revelation—the new covenant with the old, Christ the Redeemer with God the Creator. Christianity is not an altogether new and separate entity, with no connections to its roots and no relationship to the rest of the biblical kerygma. Rather, the Christian message, centered on Christ, is centered on the Word and work of God in Christ.

This is the important point. Christocentricity cannot be allowed to stand over against theocentricity, as an alternative to theocentricity. It must be seen as a form of theocentricity, namely, that which takes the Christ-event as the key to the understanding of God and God as the key to the understanding of the Christ-event. When the Christ-event is interpreted as the Word and work of God there is no conflict between Christocentricity and theocentricity.

## Proposition 3: Christian theocentricity includes all God's work and Word.

This makes explicit the wider scope of Christian faith and specifies that this faith is inclusive of all revealed truth, the entire sweep of revelation—of God's Word in any form, God's works from beginning to end. Christianity is not limited or partial in perspective; it does not simply proclaim God's work in Christ. Moreover, its Christology is not separate from its theology. On the contrary, Christology spills over into theology—gives shape, in fact, to theology—in such a way as to lead the Christian to look at all God's work, from creation to consummation, as a continuous Christ-event. The Christian believer considers Christ the universal agent in all that God says and does.

27

## Proposition 4: Christology is a continuous process of Christocentric theological reflection.

This at one and the same time indicates that Christianity has a definite identity which is marked by Christocentricity and that the Christian understanding of Christ is dynamic and developing—the result of an ongoing process of theological reflection. It is important to affirm both, so as to hold together the principal concern for the integrity and authenticity of Christian faith and the practical observation that Christian faith-reflection—even Christology—has developed through history and is in fact still developing.

It should be noted that this understanding of the nature of Christian theology is fully responsive to the basic concerns of theological orthodoxy while at the same time affirming the validity of progressive theology. In fact, it strengthens the interaction between the two. In speaking about Christian theology in terms of "the identity, integrity, and authenticity of Christian faith," we are freeing the basic concerns of orthodoxy of the overtones of static dogmatism; and in describing the ongoing theological process as "Christocentric theological reflection," we intentionally tie all new and progressive theological endeavors into continuity with the original, essential function of theology in the Christian community.

## Proposition 5: Christology takes shape in interaction with the church's life-situation.

This is to say that the Christology of the Christian community is historical and contextual, even evolutional. As Christians reflect on the implications of Christocentricity, in response to and in the light of their life-situation—including, for us, the contemporary situation, the modern understanding of the world, contemporary thought-forms, language, yes, culture as a whole—the Christian faith is updated, reformulated, expanded.

We should not be disturbed by this kind of contextual or

situational-evolutional orientation. It does not mean that Christianity itself—the Christian commitment, Christocentricity—is changed; only that the Christian community's awareness of the meaning, the implications, and the consequences of its Christocentric faith is brought into touch with the realities of life as they are and develop. Christocentricity stays constant, then, but Christology—Christocentric theological reflection—evolves and is rethought at every new stage of human history.

## Proposition 6: There is an important christological task before the Christian community today.

This says simply that we must do today what Christian believers in earlier ages have done for their day and time, namely, rethink our Christology—update our Christocentric theological reflection—in response to and in the light of our present life-situation. It indicates, in fact, that if Christians today are to be true to the traditions of the past, they must assume responsibility for advancing the Christocentric perspective in relation to the major developments in contemporary culture.

Faithfulness to the tradition does not simply mean repeating the christological reflections of the past; rather, it means to learn from our forefathers—the fathers of the church—how Christocentric theological reflection is done, and then proceed to do it in relation to the realities of contemporary existence. Theological responsibility is not limited to the analysis and representation of classical christological orthodoxy; instead, it manifests itself in the desire to learn the dynamics of christological reflection from the past and the courage to turn with the Christocentric perspective toward responsible theological reflection for today and in the future.

The last paragraph serves a double function: as a summation of our conception of the theological task, and as transition to the main concerns of this book. What we are about to do is to go back into the tradition—in fact, all the way back to the beginnings of Christian faith, where Christocentric theological reflection took its start, in the writings of the New Testament—for the purpose of learning the dynamics of Christology. We shall seek to do this in such a way as to involve ourselves in the dynamics of the christological process at each stage of its development; we shall seek to recapture and recapitulate the experiences and thought-processes through which the earliest Christians went and in which their faith came to life.

There are four specific stages in this development which are crucial to the understanding of the dynamics of Christology. Let me outline them here, before analyzing them, one by one, in the following chapters.

The *first* has to do with the Synoptic Gospels and the image they draw of the relationship between the disciples and Jesus. This is where it all started; we are dealing with the first, the beginning level of faith. The disciples were confronted with the person and work of Jesus of Nazareth—"the historical Jesus," as he was later designated. They saw him and heard him, and they believed him to be the Christ. Many others saw "and did not see," heard "and did not hear."

Christological reflection, on this level, involves being confronted with someone human and believing him to be divine, hearing and seeing something earthly and taking it to be heavenly, experiencing something common and interpreting it to be special. The point is elementary, but it is not trite; this dimension of Christology is still relevant to Christians. It teaches us the dynamics of relating faith to facts, meaning to observation; and it shows us the necessity of making a commitment and of learning to live with common history, even now.

The *second* stage of Christology has to do with the death of Jesus and the important changes that took place in the relationship between the disciples and the Christ as his presence was no longer a matter of flesh and blood, but of spirit. One can actually say that only at this stage did the faith become truly faithful; only now did faith gain the peculiar blessedness which Jesus, in anticipation, had ascribed to those "who have not seen and yet believe." "The historical Jesus" was no longer there; the apostles were no longer eyewitnesses. From now on they could only witness to "the Christ of faith." Up to now they had been observers; now they became messengers, bearers of his Word.

Christology on this second level involves more than relating faith to facts; here the Christian faith-commitment becomes a matter of spirituality, of inspiration, of "baptism in the Holy Spirit." We shall need to understand what this kind of commitment is all about; it is still relevant to Christian faith and life, and to theology, in our time.

The *third* level of christological reflection which we shall explore below has to do with the ministry of Peter and Paul and the radical opening of the gospel of Christ to the Gentile world. That this represented a new stage in the development of Christology is obvious; the Jerusalem Council in A.D. 45 was clearly conscious of that. Paul and his disciples openly claimed that Christ was not merely a Jewish Messiah; he is God's Christ to all the world. Moreover, commitment to Christ was no longer to be tied to obedience to the Jewish law and covenant; "the secret of Christ," said the Pauline school, "never before revealed to men," is that "the Gentiles," the outsiders, even the outcasts, "are fellow heirs, members of the same body, and partakers of the promise in Christ Jesus through the gospel" (Eph. 3:6).

What we see at this point in the church's development is Christology gone radical, "ecumenical," inclusive. We must make sure that we understand what this involves. We cannot understand the new covenant without it.

The *fourth* level of Christology which we shall consider relates to the vast expansion of christological reflection which took place in the early church as Christians learned to combine Jewish messianic apocalypticism with Greek philosophical perspectives, and began to look at all God's works, from beginning to end, as a single, continuous, universal Christ-event. Not only did the early Christians extend their Christology *backward*, through the historical Jesus, to the Davidic line and the Abrahamitic traditions; they also enlarged it *upward*, so to speak, identifying Christ as the preexistent Logos, the creative Word, God. This meant that the historical Jesus could now be interpreted as "God's son," "born of God," "the incarnate Word," and that his continuing presence in the spirit, following his death, could be seen as evidence of his "resurrection" and "ascension," even "the resumption of his lordship." And the early Christians expanded their Christology *forward*, as well—*out*, as we have seen, toward all the

31

world, of which Christ is seen to be the universal Redeemer, but *forward*, also, to the end of history, when all things, in the fullness of time, are "to unite . . . in him, things in heaven and things on earth" (Eph. 1:10).

Commitment to Christ, on this fourth and final level, is nothing less than Christocentric universality or universal Christocentricity—Christ seen as the center and the circumference of history, of creation as well as redemption. On this level of Christology, the broadest scope and sharpest focus of Christian faith are brought together and united into one.

We have much to learn from this. Moreover, it is at this point that we have a unique christological task of our own. With the dawn of the space age, our generation has learned to think in global and cosmic categories. Now more than ever do we need to recapture the universal dimensions of the Christian faith and dare to develop them in relation to our own situation and our vastly expanded view of the world.

## CHAPTER 2

Jesus Christ—
Faith and the Problem of Historicity

We are going back to stage one of Christian faith, to the very beginnings of christological reflection. We are dealing with the Synoptic Gospels and their image of the relationship between Jesus and his disciples.

One of the most remarkable things about the Synoptic Gospels is the honesty and realism with which they present the story of the beginnings of faith. One would have thought that the authors of these Gospels, writing anywhere from twenty to sixty years after the fact, would have taken the opportunity to clean up the record and present the apostles, even at the earlier stages of their discipleship, in somewhat more heroic and dignified terms than is the case. After all, *they* were the men with authority in the church. But the Gospel writers did nothing to support any apostolic pretention to greatness or primacy or infallibility. The beginnings of the faith are not described so as to put the apostles at the center; the central figure is Jesus of Nazareth. He is the originator of the faith. The twelve were *his* disciples, selected and called by him, taught and trained by him, guided by him through the rough points in their development, and finally left shaken to the core, their faith in shambles, at his death. It is not a pretty picture.

But with all this the Synoptic Gospels do give us a helpful record of the first, faint moves toward a Christian understanding of things—of the earliest stage in the development of Christian faith. They are helpful primarily because they seem so true to humanity and to the conditions of history. We would not have been helped much by a story of supermen coming into a superior faith in supernatural ways. A story which gives full recognition to the problematics of faith, to the difficulty of believing, is more closely related to the way most of us experience these things; this sort of honesty is much to be preferred. And this is precisely what the Synoptic Gospels give us.

When this is said, we should perhaps make sure that we understand the problem of interpreting the Gospels, and especially determining and sorting out what is historical and what is theological in them. We used to think, influenced as we were by early historical-critical approaches to biblical scholarship of the nineteenth century, that the Gospels were records—historical-factual records—that put us in touch with the originating events as they actually happened. That reading was the inspiration of the so-called "quest" of the historical Jesus, that naïve attempt to get rid of theology and mythology and penetrate to the bare facts—the biographical truth about Jesus, cleansed of all doctrinal superstructures. We have since learned, of course, primarily from the form critics of the twentieth century, that the sources we have to work with, even the Synoptic Gospels, are not strictly speaking historical records; they are more like sermons, proclaiming an interpretation of certain events and mixing together facts and interpretations, history and faith, without carefully indicating what is what. So it is difficult to determine precisely what the historical core of these sources is. The most sceptical among the form critics of the 1920s, 30s, and 40s even went so far as to say that the Gospels can give us no ground to claim that we have access to historical actualities *at all*. However, more recently a third, more balanced view of the gospels has emerged, one which teaches us to consider them "foundation stories"—stories that contain both facts and faith and that are important only because of this combination. They describe events that are foundational of faith, and they express the faithful interpretations of these events. This has brought about a new kind of biblical inquiry—what is called "redaction criticism"— designed to clarify the perspectives that are at work, whether historical or theological, among the Gospel writers. We now know that the content of the New Testament is *both* historical and theological. We no longer take *everything* as historical, the way it was done in precritical times; nor do we *sort* the material, as nineteenth-century liberalism did, into separate batches, keeping only that which is unmistakably historical and dismissing that which is obviously mythological. History and myth are *both* involved; both have meaning. Both contribute to making the New Testament the kind of book it is.

Now, when it comes to determining what is what in the New Testament text and interpreting both its history and its theology correctly, there is of course considerable difference of opinion, both among scholars and among laypersons. And no wonder. The New Testament is such a complex piece of writing, and people have so many different conceptions of what such literature is all about. For myself, I must confess that I draw the perimeters of history and fact rather narrowly. I consider historical or factual only that which is verifiable by objective observation or at least understandable, from a commonsensical point of view, to any reasonable human being. Material that goes beyond this, I take to be mythical or metaphorical, expressive of an interpretive perspective, symbolic rather than descriptive. I do *not* consider myth false or untrue simply because it is nonverifiable, or true only when it can be proven to be factual. I allow for a wide range of functions for the mythical or symbolic forms of language. The meaning expressed by way of myth is *also*, in a sense—perhaps even in a *deeper sense—true*.

Let us return to the subject: The story of the early development of faith, as we have it in the Synoptic Gospels, is clearly both theologically and historically motivated. In describing the relationship between Jesus of Nazareth and the disciples the way they did, the Gospel writers not only wanted to make the theological statement that the faith has its center in the confession that Jesus is the Christ; they wanted also to make clear what the historical-factual process was through which this faith emerged, and particularly that it dawned on the disciples only slowly, only with difficulty, and, at this stage in their life, only partially. Both of these functions of the story are important in our context. The *theological statement* makes clear that the Christian faith centers on the conviction that Jesus is the Christ, and the *historical statement* explains the dynamics of that faith commitment, how it came about. So, the Synoptic Gospels help us understand both the *content* and the *dynamics* of early Christian faith.

Now, to help us reflect further on what is being said in the Synoptic story, let me set the scene in broader outline.

Clearly, the beginnings of the relationship between Jesus and his disciples can be traced to his emergence as a preacher and his call for them to follow him. That is how the earliest Gospel, Mark, has it. No birth narrative here; no genealogy to tie Jesus in with the Davidic bloodline; no story of a twelve-year-old wonder-child conversing brilliantly with learned men in the temple. Nothing here to prove messianic status. Jesus is described as one among the many who was stirred up by the preaching of John the Baptist, baptized by him, then withdrawing like him for a time in the wilderness. When word reached him that John had been arrested, Jesus was ready to take over; he went into Galilee and began to preach, "The time is fulfilled, and the kingdom of God is at hand; repent, and believe in the gospel" (Mark 1:15). Then he called his disciples, Simon and his brother Andrew, fishermen at the sea of Galilee; James and John, also fishermen; Levi, a tax collector; and the others—Philip, Bartholomew, Thomas, another James, another Simon, Thaddaeus, and Judas. Probably all of them were baptized by John; all of them, surely, were gripped by high messianic expectations.

Apocalyptic messianism was all about them at the time—it was the cumulative effect of centuries of political and religious indignities, suffered at the hands, first of the Greeks, then of the Romans. The Greeks, one hundred seventy-five years before, had set up an altar to Zeus in the temple, demanded sacrifices, burned the Scriptures, forbidden circumcision. The Maccabees had led an early revolt, recaptured the temple, and successfully withstood these foreign pressures for a hundred years or more; but when Pompey finally brought Palestine under Roman control in 63 B.C., it was the end of Jewish independence. Palestine first became part of the Roman province of Syria, with a Jewish king serving at the pleasure of Caesar. Then the kingdom was split in three, Judah becoming a separate province governed by a Roman procurator. Finally the whole country was brought under the authority of the Roman governor in Jerusalem. But even with that the people were not hopeless. As had happened before, suppression once again fired the apocalyptic hopes of the

Jewish people. Ascetic sects sprang up. Learned men searched the scriptures. Zealots called the young to action. Pious men and women waited and prayed. All hearts and minds were tuned to any sign of deliverance. Surely, God would not desert his people! Surely, this was the time for a Messiah!

John the Baptist was a leading figure in the apocalypticism of the day. His movement swept the country. Many thought he was "the one," but he disavowed the claim. For himself he sought only the role of a messenger; he baptized with *water*; after him would come the one anointed, the Messiah, the Christ, who would baptize with *Spirit*.

The Gospels of Mark and Luke do *not* include the story, so prominent in John's Gospel, about the Baptist pointing to Jesus and saying, "This is he of whom I said, 'After me comes a man who ranks before me. . . .' 'Behold, the Lamb of God!' " (John 1:30, 36). The earliest Gospels refer to the Baptist, not to prove the messiahship of Jesus, but to set the scene within which the faith commitment could emerge that Jesus of Nazareth is the Messiah. It was later, much later, that the church learned to argue its faith-commitment by reference to objective proofs; at the beginning there were no proofs—only a carpenter's son from Nazareth who had been baptized by John and who now came forth to preach. The men he called as disciples had little to go on, no hard and fast evidence, only a challenge to follow and an invitation to become disciples—learners.

At this point a couple of troublesome themes of New Testament scholarship come into the picture, namely, the question of Jesus' *messianic self-consciousness* and the problem of the *messianic secret*. I shall not presume to solve these issues—my suspicion is that they are wrongly stated to begin with and can simply be dissolved. There is no doubt that as the Synoptic Gospel writers develop their story of the relationship between Jesus and his disciples, they describe Jesus as possessing a consciousness of messianic mission. That is clear from the story; this is what the church wanted us to know. The earliest Gospel points to his *baptism* as the moment when this consciousness dawned on Jesus. This story is of course mythical in form—containing such symbolic features as "the Spirit descending upon him like a dove; and a voice . . . from heaven, saying, 'Thou art my beloved Son; with

37

thee I am well pleased' " (which are quotations from Psalm 2 and Isaiah 42, well-known messianic passages to any pious Jew). But its meaning is not problematic. Here Jesus can be seen to undergo an experience of entering consciously into the messianic role, appropriating to himself the central traditions concerning the messianic mission. His messianic self-consciousness, from this perspective, is the result of a fundamental faith-commitment on his part.

If this understanding of the messianic self-consciousness of Jesus seems too weak, it may be because we tend to do Christology in terms of metaphysical categories concerned with divine and human "nature," "substance," "preexistence," and "incarnation"—concepts which came into vogue much later, under the impact of Greek philosophy. The Gospel of Mark was not written according to the categories of Chalcedon. By itself, the interpretation of Jesus' baptism as signifying his existential commitment to being the Christ is both sensible and valid. It also makes sense out of the curious feature in the Synoptic Gospels described as "the messianic secret."

That Jesus was reluctant to have people proclaim him as the Messiah is a theme that characterizes all three Synoptic Gospels. Mark makes it clearer perhaps than any of the others. At the opening of his story, as he describes Jesus' preaching in the synagogue at Capernaum, he talks about a man in the crowd who went into a fit and cried out, "I know who you are, the Holy One of God" (1:24). Jesus "rebuked him" and bade him be silent. A day or so later Jesus "sternly charged" a leper who had been cleansed, "See that you say nothing to any one" (1:43-44). And as the days went by and the crowds grew, and many people cried out, "You are the Son of God," Jesus "strictly ordered them not to make him known" (3:11-12). The theme is carried through, almost to the end of the story. Even at Caesarea Philippi, where the disciples first ventured the confession that he, Jesus, was the Christ, Jesus "charged them to tell no one about him" (8:30).

This is manifestly curious. But it is most puzzling—not even understandable—if one reads these stories from the perspective of classical, speculative, metaphysical Christology. It does not make sense, if Jesus was "of the substance and nature of God," "the objective manifestation of the divine presence in human form," to try to keep this quiet.

What is going on here, then? Why the messianic secret? When we interpret Jesus' messianic self-consciousness as his existential commitment to the role of the Messiah, the messianic secret itself gains a distinct purpose. It becomes: (1) *part of the process by which Jesus keeps his messiahship a matter of faith, not of observation,* and (2) *the means by which he makes sure that his own interpretation of the messianic role becomes determinative for the way his followers understand him.* Both of these points are important: His being the Messiah was not—not even to Jesus himself—a matter of fact but of commitment; and his commitment to messiahship was not to him tantamount to accepting any and all types of messianic roles. His was a particular christological commitment.

Going back now to the disciples, we can begin to comprehend what they were going through. We see *on the one hand their high messianic expectations.* Not only were these expectations high *in intensity;* they were high in *the way the Messiah was conceived,* also. Influenced as it was primarily by the books of Daniel and Enoch, the prevalent image of the Coming One was that of "the Son of man"—a heavenly being to whom was given all glory and honor, power and dominion, and one to be recognized as Lord of all the earth, preexistent and everlasting. This was what John the Baptist had talked about—the one (as he said), who is to come, "who is mightier than I, the thong of whose sandals I am not worthy to stoop down and untie," he will "baptize you with the Holy Spirit and with fire" (Mark 1:7; Luke 3:16). His coming was to be the end of the age. Final judgment was near. And fulfillment.

But then, *on the other hand, there was this man from Nazareth.* An ordinary man, from all appearance; of a background similar to their own. A Galilean carpenter's son, who was baptized by John. Suddenly he goes public and begins to preach. The kingdom, he says, is here; the time is fulfilled.

What were they to think? The contrast was simply too staggering! In order for them to be able to accept the commitment that he, Jesus of Nazareth, was Christ, the Messiah of God, the Son of man, they had to cope with several things. For *one* thing, *they had to come to terms with his humanity.* This was no minor problem. They had no difficulty imagining God's Anointed One coming in splendor and power. As long as there were signs and wonders, superhuman works and supernatural events, they could quite easily make the connection between the facts and their faith. But here was humility, limitations and powerlessness, refusal to offer signs, opposition, rejection. That was surely an elementary obstacle—his humanity. For *another, there was the problem of trying to understand his particular kind of messiahship.* This was no minor problem either. They were well acquainted with the messianic traditions. Had Jesus accepted the acclaim of the people, or had he laid plans for a political putsch that would ultimately bring him—and them—to power in Jerusalem, they would quickly have acknowledged that his appearance had fulfilled their expectations. But instead Jesus avoided popularity, predicted suffering, accepted the probability of violent death. No wonder they were puzzled.

The difficulties we are describing were not, of course, theirs alone. Any honest person must surely confess that it is difficult to confront someone human and believe him to be divine, to hear and see something earthly and take it to be heavenly, to experience something common and interpret it to be special. Lessing's famous question, "In what sense can something historical and particular ever be considered representative of the eternal and universal?" speaks very clearly of the most crucial issue of faith. Moreover, any honest believer must confess that it is difficult to harmonize the image of a "suffering servant" with that of the powerful Son of man, or to hold together the proclamation of the kingdom of God with the announcement of the impending death of the proclaimer, or to think that one has encountered the purest and the best and then see him betrayed and hunted and eventually crucified between two robbers at a dungheap outside the city. Kierkegaard's analysis of the "offense" of the gospel, of the utter "hiddenness" of this theophany, deals directly with the most central problem of Christology.

It is because of these difficulties that I said earlier the Synoptic Gospels are so helpful to us; they give an honest and realistic picture of the earliest stages in the development of the faith. Consider the following three passages:

*Mark 3:19 ff.* This is during the first few days of Jesus' ministry. The word was spreading about him; people flocked to hear him; extraordinary things were happening. People were being healed; many were amazed at his teachings. But some were shocked at what he said and did—why, he even took it upon himself to forgive sins! He ate and drank with sinners and tax collectors, all the while the Pharisees and John's disciples were fasting! And he broke the sabbath! Then Mark writes:

Then he went home; and the crowd came together again, so that they could not even eat. And when his family heard it, they went out to seize him, for people were saying, "He is beside himself." And the scribes who came down from Jerusalem said, "He is possessed by Beelzebul, and by the prince of demons he casts out the demons." . . .

And his mother and brothers came; and standing outside they sent to him and called him. And a crowd was sitting about him; and they said to him, "Your mother and your brothers are outside, asking for you." And he replied, "Who are my mother and brothers?" And looking around on those who sat about him, he said, "Here are my mother and my brothers!" (Mark 3:19-22, 31-34)

Let us mark such passages—they speak of the elementary problems of Christology. Obviously, the appearance of Jesus left room for a number of interpretations; faith did not spring unhindered into full bloom around him. Religious leaders found him possessed; his friends thought he had lost his mind; his family was puzzled by the strange metamorphosis in his identity.

*Mark 6:1 ff.* Jesus has returned home once more, following an exciting trip to the other side of the Sea of Galilee, to the land of the Gerasenes. On his way back, he amazed everyone by bringing Jairus' daughter out of a coma, back on her feet. Then this story:

And on the sabbath he began to teach in the synagogue; and many who heard him were astonished, saying, "Where did this man get all this? What is the

41

wisdom given to him? What mighty works are wrought by his hands! Is not this the carpenter, the son of Mary and brother of James and Joses and Judas and Simon, and are not his sisters here with us?" And they took offense at him. And Jesus said to them, "A prophet is not without honor, except in his own country, and among his own kin, and in his own house." And he could do no mighty work there. (Mark 6:2-5a)

Notice what is going on here—there is an interesting twist to the story. Usually we think of Jesus' miracles and mighty works as producing faith; here we find that it was *faith that was the basis of what he could do*. And there is another important point in the story: The people of the synagogue were offended, not at his teaching, and not at his mighty works, for they had always believed God's messenger would come characterized by such things. What gave them trouble was his humanity, his particularity, his family roots and social context.

*Luke 7:18 ff.* This is a story found only in Luke and Matthew. John the Baptist, then in prison, is told of the excitement surrounding Jesus. People everywhere are saying, "A great prophet has arisen among us," "God has visited his people!" But John wonders. He had been the voice in the wilderness, preparing the way; he had prophesied more cataclysmic events, the appearance of the mighty messianic king, the Son of man. Luke writes:

And John, calling to him two of his disciples, sent them to the Lord [Luke uses this title anachronistically], saying, "Are you he who is to come, or shall we look for another?" And when the men had come to him, they said, "John the Baptist has sent us to you, saying, 'Are you he who is to come, or shall we look for another?' " In that hour he cured many of diseases and plagues and evil spirits, and on many that were blind he bestowed sight. And he answered them, "Go and tell John what you have seen and heard: the blind receive their sight, and the lame walk, lepers are cleansed, and the deaf hear, the dead are raised up, the poor have good news preached to them. And blessed is he who takes no offense at me." (Luke 7:19-23)

Notice that John, Jesus' mentor, had no difficulty believing the reports he received of Jesus' mighty works. He had expected to hear such things—and more. What caused him trouble was the particularity, the limitations, the sheer humanity of what was reported to him. Was *this* the fulfillment—one of his own baptizees coming forth to preach, going about doing good, gathering about him a band of common men, sinners and outcasts? Jesus' response is also revealing: "Don't take offense at me," he said. "Don't let my humanity blind you to my mission. My appearance may not correspond to our messianic model, but my ministry and my message are surely in line with the messianic ideal. Believe me, not because of my person, but because of my message and my work."

So, the Synoptic Gospels give clear notice of the problematics of faith. No one was immune to these difficulties—the religious leaders of the country, Jesus' friends, his family, his home congregation, his major religious mentor. All of them had to come to terms with his humanity; all of them had to learn how he understood his messiahship. The disciples, selected by him to be his followers, his emissaries, his apostles, had to learn the same things.

We cannot talk about the development of the disciples' faith-commitment without considering what took place on the road to Caesarea Philippi. All the Gospels have this story—Mark and Luke in very similar form, Matthew with a few elaborations of a theological and ecclesiastical nature, and John largely rewritten, but with generally the same content. I shall use Mark's version, which is at once both the fullest and the most direct. Let me quote it:

And Jesus went on with his disciples, to the villages of Caesarea Philippi; and on the way he asked his disciples, "Who do men say that I am?" And they told him, "John the Baptist; and others say, Elijah; and others one of the prophets." And he asked them, "But who do you say that I am?" Peter answered him, "You are the Christ." And he charged them to tell no one about him.

And he began to teach them that the Son of man must suffer many things, and be rejected by the elders and the chief priests and the scribes, and be killed, and after three days rise again. And he said this plainly. And Peter took him, and began to rebuke him. But turning and seeing his disciples, he rebuked Peter, and said, "Get behind me, Satan! For you are not on the side of God, but of men." (Mark 8:27-33)

This story is pregnant with meaning—it is clearly the most important christological text in the Synoptic tradition. It has two parts, one concerned with Peter's *confession*, the other with Peter's *confusion*. The two parts underscore two essential points: That at its earliest stage, Christology involved both the confession that *Jesus is the Christ* and the affirmation that *the Christ is Jesus*.

The beautiful thing about this story is that it makes plain what actually takes place when faith evolves in the context of historical particularity and on the level of personal encounter. It explains the dynamics of the commitment to Christ; it makes clear the shape and theological content of it as well.

Look at it for a moment: Jesus asks, "Who do people say I am?" and "Who do *you* say I am?"

Why does he ask? Obviously not because he did not know who he was. He knew his own commitment to the role of the Christ. He asks in order to gauge how those around him perceived him. He wanted to know whether his own perception of his role and task was at all reflected in the understanding of his contemporaries. But why *ask?* Why not show them? Why not prove to them once and for all that he was *it?* Why leave the matter of his identity to their own judgment? The answer is simple: Had he proven it for a fact, made it indubitable to them, they would not have been believers. Had his messiahship been a matter of observation, there would have been little difference between being his follower and being his opponent—the only difference would have been that the followers acknowledged the fact, while others refused. No, he *would not* prove it. Faith was to be kept faithful. All anyone was ever to see was a man; all they would encounter was his works and his words. From then on, everything would depend on their own response.

Look at the answers: "Some say John the Baptist, others Elijah, others some other prophet." And then, Peter's confession, "You are the Christ."

Why these discrepancies? Was it not clear who he was? Obviously not. Christology, you see, is not a matter of observation; it is interpretation, faithful commitment. But why so many different interpretations? Why such different commitments? Why did they not all reach the same conclusion? Again the answer is simple: Had there been only one conclusion, one possible answer, it would not have been a matter of faith. Had the messiahship of Jesus been a logical proposition, there would have been no real difference between being a believer and being an unbeliever—the only difference would have been that believers affirmed the proposition, while others denied it. No, there *had to be* different answers. The response would have to be based on commitment. *He* was there, Jesus of Nazareth, right before their eyes; but the *meaning* of his life, his christological status, could only be recognized in an act of decisive commitment and expressed in confessional language.

Look at Jesus' response. Immediately, as the christological commitment is expressed, he proceeds to teach them what is involved—that they must expect to see him suffer, to be rejected, and ultimately to be killed. "You must understand," he seems to say, "that the Son of man is not here in heavenly form, in power and glory; he is more like a suffering servant. That at least is how *I* conceive my christological role."

Why did he go into this? Why throw cold water on their enthusiasm? They had come to believe that Jesus was the Christ; why not leave the rest open? The answer, once again, is simple: Had he not specified the shape and content of his own conception of the messianic role, the disciples would soon have become puzzled by the discrepancies between *their* image of the Christ and *his*. They would have believed that Jesus was the Christ, but they would probably have questioned whether the Christ really was what Jesus turned out to be. Their tendency, you see, was to interpret the Christ in terms of popular Jewish apocalypticism—the Son of man, when he came, would restore the people of God, inaugurate a new age, issue judgment over all God's enemies, and rule in the power and glory of God! Their confession that Jesus was the Christ gives an indication that they had managed to overcome the initial shock of his humanity; but they were still apparently thinking that he had the makings of greatness, that out of these inauspicious beginnings would emerge the kingdom of God as they had dreamed of and anticipated it. Jesus could not allow this to go unchecked. The christological model *he* had in mind was inspired by other traditions—most deeply the prophetic tradition, and especially the servant songs in the Book of Isaiah. That was where he had found his text when he first stepped forward to declare himself in the synagogue at Nazareth (Luke 4:16 ff); that was where his own views and expectations were anchored. He *had* to make sure that his own disciples saw his messiahship the way he did.

Look finally at the closing exchange between Peter and Jesus. Having learned how Jesus envisioned the future, Peter took him aside "and began to rebuke him." Matthew has him say, "God forbid, Lord! This shall never happen to you." Then Jesus rebukes Peter: "Get behind me, Satan! For you are not on the side of God, but of men" (Mark 8:33).

That is certainly a strange thing to say. Moments after Peter made the great confession he is suddenly identified with the enemy of God! Why such dogmatism? Peter had seen the light; why not listen to him and affirm him? The answer is clear: Not every faith-commitment is a Christian commitment; not every interpretation of the Christ is the Christian interpretation. There is a *norm* laid down for Christology, and that norm is Jesus' self-interpretation. Jesus' own understanding of his messiahship is the criterion by which all his followers' faith-commitments must be tested. The fact that Peter one moment makes a true confession and is called blessed, while the next moment he goes wrong and is rebuked, only goes to show that faith is a precarious venture. Correctness at one point does not guarantee orthodoxy throughout. There is no infallibility in faith, not even in Peter's.

So the faith-commitment to Christ stands or falls on its correspondence with the christological commitment of Jesus. He is the originator and the fulfiller of the faith. As for Peter, he obviously had a lot to learn, still. But that's our subject for the next chapter.

Let me add one bibliograhical note.

If the dynamics of faith which I have outlined here has particular interest to any reader, let me encourage further exploration of two books: first, Sören Kierkegaard's penetrating study of the relationship between Jesus and his disciples in *Training in Christianity* (Princeton University Press, 1944); second, Hans Küng's *On Being a Christian*.

The first is a classic, of theology as well as personal devotion, and the christological sections of Küng's work will, in spite of everything his opponents among the German bishops may say, surely come to be recognized as one of the most enlightened contributions to the modern understanding of Christ and the Christian message.

## CHAPTER 3

## *Christus Spiritus*—Faith and
## the Breakthrough to Spirituality[1]

We come now to the second level of christological reflection apparent in the New Testament—the second stage in the development of Christian faith—namely, that which emerged following the death of Jesus, when the relationship between his followers and him no longer was one of historical presence, flesh and blood, but of memory and spirit. A tremendous change took place at this point, both in the way the apostolic community *experienced* the faith-commitment and in the way they *understood the meaning* of the Christ-event. There developed, in fact, an entirely new dynamics of faith; and there emerged, as a result, a dramatically new Christology. We need to be quite clear about what happened.

Let me pull the string and spill the beans—I shall have plenty of time to chase them down and try to bring them back together in the end, anyway.

I want to profess an impression which has grown stronger within me for the last ten to twelve years, primarily as the result of renewed studies in the New Testament: The most inadequately understood part of the gospel, the most superficially acknowledged dimension of Christian faith and experience generally, is connected with Pentecost. This goes for those among us who consider the story of Pentecost so full of obscure first-century mythology—"tongues as of fire," "sound . . . like the rush of a mighty wind," and such—that it is virtually useless as model for Christian experience today. And it goes for those in our midst as well who call themselves "pentecostalists" and "charismatics" and who not only take the story of Pentecost literally, but also proceed on its basis to develop an elaborate spiritualistic mythology of their own. The first group is likely to miss the deeper meaning of this part of Christian faith and experience altogether, and the second group, I am sad to say, seems satisfied with the recapitulation of the outward characteristics of the experience and remains generally unwilling or unable to explore what is actually involved, theologically and experientially.

Pentecost has, in fact, fallen upon evil days. Among the great festivals of the church year, it is clearly the least understood and the most ignored. Traditionally, the church celebrated this day as the commemoration of the "descent" of the Spirit—that dynamic, inspiring Presence within the faith and life of early Christians which was seen to have constitutive importance in the formation of the church itself. In our time, much more attention seems to be given a "founders day," when we commemorate the organizational beginnings of our congregations, or a "homecoming," when the whole church family comes together to enjoy its own food and fellowship. Pentecost is something of a stepchild among the seasons of faith. Check the services and sermon topics in most churches on the seventh Sunday after Easter and you will find surprisingly few congregations being given the opportunity to venture into this particular part of the church's annual liturgical pilgrimage through the faith. Ask any average layman what Pentecost is all about and you will find in his answer an illustration of the second verse in the Bible—"The earth was without form and void, and darkness was upon the face of the deep" (Gen. 1:2*a*).

Not much better, I am sad to say, is the fate of Pentecost among contemporary spiritual enthusiasts who tend to lay monopolistic claims to the experience of the Holy Spirit and who take this experience to be authentic only when it conforms to every outward feature in the New Testament foundation story. Ask a typical charismatic what Pentecost *means*, and you receive answers, almost universally, that are cast either in terms of purely subjective, even emotional states, or consist of noninterpreted symbolic phrases such as "baptism of the Holy Spirit," "gift of the Holy Spirit." When these phrases go unexplained and without reference to what actually takes place, they are altogether circular and nonexplanatory, meaningful only to those who are used to this mythology, and then only in a limited sense.

My professed conviction is that Pentecost is the most *inadequately* understood part of the gospel and the most *superficially* acknowledged dimension of Christian faith and experience. This is the negative side of a positive point that has come to have the force of a new discovery for me, namely, that as far as the New Testament is concerned, it was at Pentecost that the faith became truly faithful, that the commitment to Christ became truly commitmental. No other experience plays a comparable role in the development of the disciples' faith. It was at Pentecost—not by the river Jordan, not by the Sea of Galilee, not on the Mount of Transfiguration, not at the cross, not even at the open grave—it was at Pentecost that the disciples finally crossed the line and became Christ's apostles. Up to that point they had been wavering and floundering, oscillating between clarity and confusion, insight and blindness, shifting back and forth between faith and doubt, spirituality and worldly thinking. At Pentecost, that was all changed. They reached a new, a deeper level of commitment and faith.

What happened to these people? I mean, *what was it that actually took place* behind the odd symbolism of the Pentecost story, the "sound . . . like the rush of a mighty wind," "tongues as of fire," and all the rest? Perhaps if we understood that, we would not only gain a greater appreciation for this part of the Christian tradition; we might in fact come to understand more deeply what Christian faith and life is all about for ourselves, today.

In order to get at the meaning of Pentecost, I propose that we go, not to the story as recorded in the book of Acts, but to a piece of theological reflection found in Paul's Second Letter to the Corinthians:

The love of Christ controls us, beause we are convinced that one has died for all; therefore all have died. And he died for all, that those who live might live no longer for themselves but for him who for their sake died and was raised.

From now on, therefore, we regard no one from a human point of view; even though we once regarded Christ from a human point of view, we regard him thus no longer. Therefore, if any one is in Christ, he is a new creation; the old has passed away, behold, the new has come. (II Cor. 5:14-17)

"From now on," he says, "the new has come." What was the *old*, and what is the *new*, and what is this *now* of transition?

Paul gives clear directions toward answering such questions. The *old* is obviously the common human point of view, the worldly way of looking at things, or as he expresses it, looking at things *kata sarka*, "according to the flesh." He indicates that even Christ can be considered from this perpective—that is, historically, factually, commonsensically. But it is an *old* perspective. There is, of course, historicity and facticity involved in Christology; Paul has no doubts whatever about that. The human existence of the man Jesus of Nazareth can be ascertained historically. The historical Jesus was not a fluffy myth, in Paul's estimation; he was a real man, solid flesh, red blood. But to emphasize this is not really all that significant for Paul, particularly not after Jesus' historical death. If the factual assertion— or even description—of his historicity was all one could say about him, then one's reason for talking would now have passed away; one's relationship to him would have been brutally broken by his death.

It is here that a *new* point of view must be found. And it can be. Says Paul, "From now on . . . we regard no one from a human point of view." What is the new perspective? Paul indicates that it has to do with an inward or existential awareness of identification with Christ—a relationship of mutual love and self-giving. It is obviously a "responsive" or commitmental stance, a commitment to a spiritual view of things, to a consideration of Christ *kata pneuma*, "according to the Spirit." It takes the historical facts about Jesus—even the most drastic fact of all, his cruel death on the cross—and finds them all pregnant with spiritual meaning. The cross, for instance, is no longer a frightful sign of tragedy and obliteration; it is the symbol of Christ's vicarious self-giving for us, on our behalf, for our redemption. In his new way of seeing things, Paul could look the ugly fact straight in the face and say, "He died, for me, and such love and sacrifice demands my life, my soul, my all!" That was the *new* which had come to

51

replace the *old*: a new way of looking at things, and a new way of life to go with it.

But how did he find it? What was the *now* that set the limit to the old and marked his transition to the new? Paul calls it conviction—"We are convinced," he says. In other contexts he talks of "conversion," using the Greek word *metanoia*, which means, "to have a new mind." What he is talking about, obviously, is a radical change of perspective, a new way of looking at things. In calling it "conviction," he is indicating that it has to do with something inward, something decisive, something spiritual. It is of the order of a new commitment. The transition from the old to the new is a fundamental changeover from outward observation, looking at things "according to the flesh," to inward appropriation, looking at things "according to the Spirit." Specifically, in regard to the relationship to Christ, it was a move from the past preoccupation with the historical Jesus to a present participation in the Christ of faith. It was to have the gospel of Christ internalized, "inspired" into one's own being. As Paul expresses it, from the moment of his conversion, he was himself "in Christ," and Christ "in him."

Is this a clue? Was it something like this that happened in the early Christian community as the disciples struggled to come to terms with the death of Jesus?

Let us look a little closer at the larger story of their developing faith, to see if we can uncover more clearly how they moved from the *old* to the *new*, and what precisely was the *now* of their transformation.

The story of the disciples' relationship to Christ—the description of the stages in the development of their commitment—was of course written after the fact, at a distance of several decades and in retrospect from the point of view which characterized the writers. This, quite naturally, has had significant influence on the story itself. The New Testament does not give the kind of straight recording of historical events which intends simply to describe what took place as it happened. The New Testament writers are theologically motivated. They write history backward, from the point of view of faith. They mix together facts and interpretation, history and proclamation. In describing the earliest stage in the development of the disciples' commitment to Christ as they do, these writers clearly wanted to indicate that the faith of the disciples was partial, incomplete, unfinished. They were beginning a journey, but they were not yet there.

Take the picture of the disciples which we find in the Synoptic Gospels.

At the time of their call to discipleship, Jesus is reported to have used the phrase, "Follow me and I will make you become fishers of men" (Mark 1:17). We recognize the appropriateness of the formulation. They were chosen, not because of what they were, but in view of what he could make them. Surely, if those men were to *become* anything at all, they would have to *learn* it from him.

There was first a period of initial instruction, when they were given the rudiments of the message of the kingdom and an initial awareness of the needs of the people. With this beginner's lesson behind them, they were sent out, two by two, on Jesus' behalf. They came back with great enthusiasm. People had listened to them; they had seen some marvelous things happening. But Jesus reminded them, "Don't get blown up by success."

"A disciple is not above his teacher, nor a servant above his master; it is enough for the disciple to be like his teacher, and the servant like his master. If they have called the master of the house Beelzebul, how much more will they malign those of his household." (Matt. 10:24-25)

After this, Jesus' teaching took on a new dimension. There was time for greater depth and a sharper edge. He spoke in parables, and the disciples were confused. "Why do you speak to them in parables?" they asked. He said:

"This is why I speak to them in parables, because seeing they do not see, and hearing they do not hear, nor do they understand. With them indeed is fulfilled the prophecy of Isaiah which says:

'You shall indeed hear but never understand, and you shall indeed see but never perceive. . . .' But blessed are your eyes, for they see, and your ears, for they hear." (Matt. 13:13-16)

But the disciples did *not* understand. Time and again they had to ask him to explain the parables. Disappointed, Jesus said to them, "Then are you also without understanding?" (Mark 7:18).

Jesus at times was hard on the Pharisees, and the disciples became flustered. "Do you know that the Pharisees were offended when they heard this saying?" they asked him. He answered, "Let them alone; they are blind guides. And if a blind man leads a blind man, both will fall into a pit" (Matt. 15:14). "Well," said Peter, "here you go with one of those parables again; explain this parable to us." There is a distinct note of frustration and impatience in Jesus' words as he answered, "Are you also [*still*] without understanding?"

There are other such expressions of disappointment on his part. After the mountaintop experience described as the Transfiguration, Jesus came back to find them with a sick boy, standing around arguing, not knowing what to do. And he said to them. "O faithless and perverse generation, how long am I to be with you? How long am I to bear with you?" (Matt. 17:17).

"Perverse," he said. It is not too strong a word. They began to discuss among themselves who would be the greatest in the kingdom; he said to them, "Unless you turn and become like children, you will never enter the kingdom of heaven" (Matt. 18:3). They pushed aside a group of mothers and children pressing around Jesus to obtain his blessing; he snapped at them indignantly, "Don't you see! These are precisely the ones whose Kingdom it is!" (cf. Mark 10:14 ff.) They were impressed when a rich young ruler came to seek Jesus' advice, and amazed when Jesus sent him away, saying, "How hard it will be for those who have riches to enter the kingdom of God! . . . It is easier for a camel to go through the eye of a needle than for a rich man to enter the kingdom of God" (Mark 10:23-25). At that they threw up their arms, and said, "Who can get in?" And Peter said, "Lo, we have left everything and followed you." Jesus answered, "But many that are first will be last and the last first" (Mark 10:28-31). Then two of them, James and John, went to him privately and said to him:

"Teacher, we want you to do for us whatever we ask of you." And he said to them, "What do you want me to do for you?" And they said to him, "Grant us to sit, one at your right hand and one at your left, in your glory." But Jesus said to them, "You do not know what you are asking. Are you able to drink the cup that I drink, or to be baptized with the baptism with which I am baptized?"

## FAITH AND THE BREAKTHROUGH TO SPIRITUALITY

And they said to him, "We are able." And Jesus said to them, "The cup that I drink you will drink; and with the baptism with which I am baptized, you will be baptized; but to sit at my right hand or at my left is not mine to grant, but it is for those for whom it has been prepared." (Mark 10:35-40)

It was like that, it seems, throughout. Never did these men seem to get a hold of what it was all about. Jesus talked of his suffering; they said, "God forbid! That must never happen!" He talked of them falling away; Peter said, "Even if they all fall away, I will not!"

But he did. He even swore with an oath that he did not know this man Jesus. He watched him die from a distance.

How did these people ever find the *new*, when they were so solidly stuck in the *old?* How did they ever break through to understanding in relation to Christ? Well, there are some pointers here and there, statements that keep recurring and that promise something more, something different.

Let me quote some selected passages from the farewell speeches of Jesus in the Gospel of John:

"I did not say these things to you from the beginning, because I was with you. But now I am going to him who sent me. . . . But because I have said these things to you, sorrow has filled your hearts. Nevertheless I tell you the truth: it is to your advantage that I go away, for if I do not go away, the Counselor will not come to you; but if I go, I will send him to you." (16:4b-7)

"I have yet many things to say to you, but you cannot bear them now. When the Spirit of truth comes, he will guide you into all the truth." (16:12-13a)

"I will not leave you desolate; I will come to you. Yet a little while, and the world will see me no more, but you will see me; because I live, you will live also. In that day you will know that I am in my Father, and you in me, and I in you." (14:18-20)

"The Counselor, the Holy Spirit, whom the Father will send in my name, he will teach you all things, and bring to your remembrance all that I have said to you." (14:26)

"He will not speak on his own authority, but whatever he hears he will speak. . . . He will glorify me, for he will take what is mine and declare it to you." (16:13-14)

I have said these were pointers, promises of something more, something different; they are actually pointers toward Pentecost. And there are many more of them, at various points in the story—in fact, the whole story seems to be written with Pentecost in mind:

"Behold, I send the promise of my Father upon you; but stay in the city, until you are clothed with power from on high." (Luke 24:49)

He charged them not to depart from Jerusalem, but to wait for the promise of the Father, which, he said, "you heard from me, for John baptized with water, but before many days you shall be baptized with the Holy Spirit." (Acts 1:4-5)

"You shall receive power when the Holy Spirit has come upon you; and you shall be my witnesses. . . ." (Acts 1:8)

There is enough here to make any reader of the New Testament want to look seriously at what this promise refers to, what this "baptism in the Holy Spirit" means, and what this "power" is which is said to go with it. We clearly need a way to unlock these symbols, to break open the outer shell so we can learn what the inner meaning is. We need to understand, in terms of actualities of human experience, what the nature of Pentecost is.

We began this process a moment ago, as we looked at Paul's statement concerning the *old* and the *new* and the *from now on* which marked the transition from one to the other, and considered them a clue. Let us see if we can make a similar analysis of John's statements, those we just quoted. I want to identify three specific emphases in these passages.

There is first the curious reference to it being to their "advantage" that Jesus "go away," for if he does not go away, "the Counselor" will not come to them. There are those, of course, who interpret the advantage reference as having to do with the Atonement, the saving significance of his death. I find it more logical to tie the reference to Jesus' going and the Counselor's coming together, and to consider them both as having to do with the radical change that would take place in the disciples' relationship to Christ now that his physical presence was coming to an end. Up to now, they had been eye-witnesses. They had been followers of Jesus, observing his works and hearing his words; and they had believed, against all appearances, that he was the Christ of God. To them, his going was a crushing blow. He had been present; now he would be absent. But in preparing them in advance for that absence, Jesus announces that his going is an advantage to them; this is because something dramatically new will happen; a different kind of Presence will be realized among them. No longer will their relationship to Christ be related to the flesh and blood, the humanity and particularity of Jesus of Nazareth; from now on the Presence of Christ will be realized, universally as well as personally, spiritually. Earlier they had seen him and believed; now they would not see him, yet believe. Earlier his presence had been external; now it would be internal. Earlier their commitment to Christ had been focused on the Christ in Jesus; now their commitment to Christ would have as its focus the spirit of Christ within. Or in Paul's language: They had known him *kata sarka*; from now on they would know him *kata pneuma*.

There is second that emphasis in the Johannine passages designed to clarify *how* this sense of presence, this internalization of the Spirit of Christ, is *actually realized* in the life of believers, namely, by way of *remembrance* and *clarification* of the message of Jesus. It is specifically stressed that the Counselor, the Holy Spirit, has no other function than to glorify Christ. He does not speak on his own authority; he takes what he teaches from what Christ has said, and he declares it; he brings into remembrance the message of Jesus, and he clarifies it. From this perspective the Holy Spirit is none other than the Spirit of Christ, or as we might well say, the spirit of Jesus—i.e., the *meaning* of his message, life, and death, made *present, clear, and true* to the believer. This, then, gives us a clue to what Christian spirituality is all about. It is the inspiration, the spiriting within of the message and meaning of Christ. What we call "the experience of the Holy Spirit" is really a deeper, more meaningful experience of Christ; what is termed "the baptism of the Holy Spirit" is in reality the entry into a new, more personal commitment to Christ.

A third emphasis in the farewell speeches of Jesus that is important in this context has to do with the indication that there is *some new truth, some greater knowledge of Christ, to be revealed to believers.* Not only will the Counselor remind them of what Jesus had said, and declare or clarify its meaning; he will guide them "into all the truth," "teach [them] all things." Jesus' statement actually contains an explicit recognition of what we might call "progressive revelation." "I have yet many things to say to you," he says, "but you cannot bear them now. When the Spirit of truth comes, he will guide you into all truth" (John 16:12-13a). Jesus even gives an indication of what this new, or greater, knowledge or truth is all about; it has to do with Christology: "I did not say these things to you from the beginning, because I was with you. But now I am going to him who sent me. . . . In that day you will know that I am in my Father, and you in me, and I in you." Two or three important christological developments are referred to in this statement: "I am going to him who sent me" is a cryptic reference to the resurrection and the ascension; "in that day you will know that I am in my Father" has reference both to the sonship and the lordship of Christ; and "you in me, and I in you" seems to have reference both to Christ-mysticism and to the vicarious, representative ministry of the apostles on behalf of Christ. We see, then, that the new, spiritual perspective which was to come was not to be limited to the retrospective clarification of the message and meaning of Jesus; Pentecost would also be the basis for a progressive, expansive Christology in the future.

Now, if in the light of such Pauline and Johannine statements, or such analysis of the dynamics of the Pentecostal experience, we should take another look at the story of the disciples' experience at Pentecost as we have it in the Book of Acts, we will discover exactly the same kind of dynamics. There is no doubt that a dramatic change was taking place in the disciples' relationship to Christ; there is no doubt either that their Christology was going through a radical expansion.

Look at Peter, for example, the very same man who at Caesarea Philippi had taken Jesus aside to tell him all this talk of suffering and death must at all cost be avoided—nothing, pardon the pun, could be more deadly to faith. Now, *at Pentecost*, he stands forth and proclaims an entirely new interpretation of these things. Listen to him:

> "Men of Israel [he says], hear these words: Jesus of Nazareth, a man attested to you by God with mighty works and wonders and signs . . . this Jesus, delivered up according to the definite plan and foreknowledge of God, you crucified and killed by the hands of lawless men. But God raised him up, having loosed the pangs of death, because it was not possible for him to be held by it. . . .
>
> "This Jesus God raised up, and of that we are all witnesses. Being therefore exalted at the right hand of God, and having received from the Father the promise of the Holy Spirit, he has poured out this which you now see and hear. . . . [Therefore] let all the house of Israel . . . know assuredly that God has made him both Lord and Christ, this Jesus whom you crucified." (Acts 2:22-24, 32-36)

What a transformation this was! Peter's old confusions were entirely gone. Here was a man with a new faith-commitment, a new message to proclaim, an understanding of Christ both deeper and higher than he had ever had before. At last Peter had come to understand the gospel of Christ; finally the meaning of it all had dawned on him. At this point, for the first time, all that he had heard and seen and learned in his sojourn with Jesus of Nazareth fell into place and made sense. Up to this moment, he had been an observer, only occasionally seeing things in faith; now he had become a participant, convinced and committed, "inspired" by Christ in his own being. The *old*, the human point of view, was left behind; from now on the *new* had come—he was looking at things according to the Spirit.

And with this we see how Peter's Christology exploded into a remarkable display of kerygmatic fireworks. Not only was the significance and meaning of Jesus' life and work "attested . . . by God"; his suffering and death were seen as part of God's own eternal plan and purpose, as well. And Peter did not stop there; he went on to proclaim that as surely as he had been an eyewitness to the Christ in the flesh, he was now a witness to the Christ in the Spirit. The death of Jesus was not the end of Christ; God had raised him up, yes, exalted him at his own right hand and made him both Lord and Christ!

This, then, is the dynamics and meaning of Pentecost. It was the moment when the followers of Jesus finally got over their preoccupation with the historical Jesus—and especially with the tragic events which marked the end of his physical presence among them. It was the moment when they finally broke through to a personal conviction of the continuing presence of Christ in the Spirit. It was the moment when they finally were able to set the Christ-event they had been a part of into the larger context of God's eternal plan and purpose, God's mighty works from beginning to end. Pentecost, in short, marks the emergence of a new commitment to Christ on the part of the disciples, an understanding of the Christ-event that goes both deeper and higher than anything they had grasped before. And it set in motion certain developments, both in regard to apostolic ministry and in regard to theology, which we shall need to look at next. These are the subjects of the next two chapters.

One other point, here at the end. Some of you may be puzzled as to how I can think of analyzing the Pentecostal experience of the disciples without considering the one item which seems so central to the whole experience and which is so much on the minds of pentecostalists and charismatics today, namely, the phenomenon of speaking "in other tongues," what is called "glossolalia."

Let me say this about that subject: I accept the fact that speaking in other tongues is part of the Pentecost story and that the gift of tongues is listed among the spiritual gifts referred to by Paul, and is a valid spiritual experience. But I think that it represents *a misunderstanding of the nature of the Pentecostal experience—indeed of Christian spirituality itself—to consider the phenomenon of speaking in tongues essential to this experience and central to spiritual life as such.* For one thing, none of the statements in the Gospels that point toward Pentecost give any reference to glossolalia as having any part in the experience at all. Second, the Pentecost story, as we have it in the Book of Acts, refers to speaking in other tongues only as a *consequence* of the fullness of the Holy Spirit, not as the essence of it, and only in connection with the function of ministry, the proclamation of the gospel to people of other language backgrounds, not as something that has reference to the quality of spirituality as such. Third, it may in fact be necessary to distinguish between what is called "speaking in other tongues" in the Pentecost story and the phenomenon of glossolalia, the so-called "gift of tongues" to which Paul refers in his list of spiritual gifts. The first was clearly a means of communicating with *other people*, outsiders; the second—as Paul says—"speaks not to men but to *God*" (1 Cor. 14:2). Fourth, the New Testament as a whole speaks of Christian spirituality and spiritual gifts in ways that are manifestly more inclusive and wide-ranging; it clearly does not put speaking in tongues either at the center of spiritual life or at the top of the list of spiritual gifts.

Be that as it may. To close with a more positive consideration of the phenomenon, allow me to quote myself—a process of steadily diminishing returns, I know, but on this point I have yet to find any better way of saying what I have in mind. I shall include two passages, one from my little book on *Advent-Christmas* in the Fortress Press Proclamation Series, another from an article entitled "A New Syntax for Religious Language" published in *Theology Today*.

The first is a reflection on the lectionary texts for Second Sunday after Christmas, particularly the Old Testament text, the Zion songs from Isaiah 61 and 62:

Characteristic of the Zion poems, as the above exegesis indicates, is the richness of imagery through which the prophet expresses his people's response to the message of redemption. From a variety of life contexts, all of them marked by celebration and joy, the prophet picks up images of festivity. Two in particular preoccupy him, namely, the wedding feast and the renewal of nature in spring—both occasions of overwhelming emotional excitement. We see the bridegroom "decking himself with a garland" and the bride "adorning herself with her jewels" (v. 10). Images and application intertwine as the poet describes being "clothed with the garments of salvation" and "covered with the robe of righteousness." We see the earth "bringing forth its shoots" and gardens "causing what is sown to spring up" (v. 11), and we are immediately told that likewise "God will cause righteousness and praise to spring forth before all nations." Magnificent—that's the word—magnificent is all that the Lord God does, and the prophet who sees it cannot and "will not keep silent" about it (62:1). He will sing about it until the meaning of it "goes forth as brightness," "as a burning torch."

Obviously, the prophet is attempting to say what his words can hardly express. He is overwhelmed with the awareness of it all, and he rejoices, playing with words, exulting in images which are more like ejaculations of a freed spirit. We ought not to be surprised at this—or at the next step that may occur, namely, the complete explosion of all normalized language and the shattering of its fragments in an emotional fireworks of *glossolalia*. Ecstasy is not an unknown experience among those that have discovered the magnitude of the gospel. Normally, of course, we do not feel things that strongly. Many among us have closed ourselves to any notion of celebration—concepts like "the dancing God" or "the feast of fools" are repulsive to us simply because they go beyond the cool rationality of our institutional religiosity. But there is still the possibility of a heart-warming breakthrough to the *fullness of the spirit*, to the overwhelming awareness of what has really taken place in and with the events which we have observed and acknowledged. And perhaps the level of exultation which we experience now is a direct corollary to the level of intensity with which we went through Advent.[2]

The second passage is from a different context—more analytical and theoretical, "methodological," if you will—but it makes a case for glossolalia as a dimension of religious language:

I am thinking of *glossolalia, speaking in tongues*. To most of us, quite naturally, this type of speech is not really language at all. It has few of the characteristics of understandable articulation and cannot, therefore, easily be accepted as a valid means of communication among rational human beings. That seems fairly clear on the surface, and therewith the matter is also settled for most people. Glossolalia is "way out" as speech goes, useless for communication purposes, and it might as well be forgotten in a modern day.

But there are some who disagree. To them, what is usually called rational speech, even the more advanced understanding of language as a revelational word event, is much too stale and unpliable a material to facilitate the free flow of the divine spirit. Furthermore, man himself is not seen simply as a "reasonable" being. He is a totality of many things, and the interplay of the Spirit of God and the spirit of man is by no means exhausted in previously arranged words and phrases, in language neatly fitted together according to accepted rules of grammar, sentence structure, and logic. The spirit may, in fact, be hindered by the restrictions involved in such matters. What is needed are some further linguistic tools to express the larger dimensions of spiritual confrontation and the deeper levels of man's person and experience, "a language" that has as rich a repertoire of sound as the Spirit of God has of influence and the spirit of man has of feeling and awareness and sensitivity. Let be that this "language" is largely an emotive experimentation in sound. Let be that the sounds are untraditional and uncontrolled and crude. But are they not still understandable?

That is the crucial question involved. The answer to that question will decide one's attitude to the phenomenon of glossolalia, and it in turn depends to a very large extent on the criteria one lays down for evaluating human understanding. One can define understanding *narrowly* in terms of rational perception and clear conceptualization and thereby exclude the emotive, tonal articulation of glossolalia from the ranks of understandable communication altogether. Or one can *widen* one's concept of human understanding to include elements of a pre-rational, meta-empirical, holistic-personal sort and thereby open the possibility of accepting into the spectrum of religious speech even a pneumatic meta-language which carries little resemblance to normal human articulation at all. The fact that most people rely on unquestioned rationalistic axioms to evaluate human understanding and human speech ought not, of course, to scare the wits out of us when we hear and see things that do not quite comply. There may be more under the sun than common words can contain, and, if so, one should not regret that people look for something else—something more—by which to give expression to the awareness of it.[3]

## CHAPTER 4

Christic for the World—
The Radical Inclusiveness of the Gospel

Our subject here has to do with yet another stage in the development of New Testament Christology, namely, the point where the commitment to Christ breaks out of its attachment to Jewish messianic traditions and manifests itself in the form of a totally new view of the work of Christ and the meaning of the gospel. We are dealing with the ministry of Peter and Paul and their leadership in the move to open the gospel of Christ to the Gentile world. What we see at this point is the commitment to Christ gone radical, inclusive, ecumenical—it has to do with the whole inhabited world.

Let me set the scene.

We are in the period of what is called "Hellenistic Jewish Mission Christianity." The apostolic community, galvanized by the break-through to a new spiritual awareness and an unapologetic resurrection faith at Pentecost, was initiating an aggressive evangelistic campaign, spreading from Jerusalem, to Judea and Samaria, "to the ends of the [then known] world." The channels through which this campaign spread were to a large extent the network of Jewish communities which had developed throughout the Greco-Roman world ever since the time of Alexander the Great—in Asia Minor (now Turkey); on the island of Cyprus; in Greece and Italy; and in North Africa, and even Spain. Everywhere the Jews had gone they had organized synagogues; and it was these synagogues that became the points of contact for the apostles as they traveled far and wide to preach Christ and make disciples. Not only were there in these synagogues Jews faithful to Judaism, and Jews open to Christianity; there were also Gentile converts to Judaism. And on the fringes were Gentile "seekers,"

"God-fearers"—Greeks and Romans open to Judaism, and many of them responsive to the gospel of Christ as well. Thus, in the initial stages of the apostles' campaign, identifiable groups of believers developed in a great many synagogues. In some places the synagogues actually split right down the middle, and Christian believers moved out and set up their own congregations.

These developments were not of course altogether peaceful and harmonious. There were persecutions everywhere—in Jerusalem, where the rulers, elders, and scribes arrested Peter and John and charged them "not to speak or teach at all in the name of Jesus" (Acts 4:18), and where Stephen was killed, as well as in many of the other communities and synagogues where the faith found roots. Saul, a Pharisee from Tarsus, a man with the best possible credentials both of background and training, became known as a leader in the campaign to rid the Jewish synagogues of the Christian influence.

Saul's development is of course an integral part of the story we are trying to trace. Raised in a devout Jewish family and brought up in the Hellenistic environment of Tarsus, he was in many ways the model representative of Hellenistic Judaism. Tarsus was an important cultural, educational, and commercial center. Here Saul received his education in the formal Greek arts, philosophy, and rhetoric. And he was educated in Jerusalem, at the feet of Gamaliel, a famous Jewish theologian and teacher, as well. He became a Pharisee—a strict legalist, a purist in regard to Jewish faith and life. He was highly skilled in rabbinical exegesis. Indications are that he became a rabbi, perhaps even a Jewish missionary in the Hellenistic context, "preaching circumcision" as he himself intimates in a later context (Gal. 5:11).

Preaching circumcision was not an easy task. Greeks generally proved to be quite open to Judaism, but not to circumcision. This was for them—no pun intended—clearly the sore spot in the Jewish message. Many simply became God-fearers, without actually converting to Judaism. It may have been at this point that the presence of Christians began to bother Saul. They preached a gospel without circumcision, salvation simply by faith in Christ. Their message was attractive to the God-fearers; to Saul, on the other hand, it must have appeared as unfair competition, a threat to the purity of Judaism. So he became a persecutor—among other things obtaining the official sanction of the high priest in Jerusalem for a vigorous move to purge the synagogues at Damascus of this influence and bring anybody found belonging to the Way in ropes to Jerusalem. It was while he was on the way there that Saul experienced his dramatic conversion, saw the light, found the faith in Christ, and was transformed from a persecutor to a radical proponent of the Christian gospel. Scholars now date Paul's conversion—and his new name—to within a year or two of the crucifixion, or about A.D. 32.

Upon his conversion, Paul was immediately contacted by the believers at Damascus and baptized to the confession, "Christ is Lord." Then he surprised everyone by going into the synagogues, proclaiming Jesus as the Son of God, confounding "the Jews who lived in Damascus by proving that Jesus was the Christ" (Acts 9:22). In his own record of these developments, Paul says that he went away immediately into Arabia (Gal. 1:17). We do not know for how long. At any rate, for a period of three years he apparently had his headquarters at Damascus, until the Jews there finally had enough of him and plotted to kill him. His friends got wind of it, helped him over the wall by night, and Paul found his way to Jerusalem, where he tried to join the disciples. But they were afraid of him; obviously, they did not believe he was really one of them.

As Paul describes it, he spent only fifteen days in Jerusalem on this visit, seeing no one but Peter, until Barnabas took care of him, brought him to the apostles, and he was allowed to confess his faith among them. But the Hellenistic Jews, his earlier compatriots, again plotted to kill him, so the apostles packed him off to Caesarea, and from there by ship to Tarsus, where he went into hiding, spending the next ten years or so in obscurity, as a tentmaker.

At this time, several new developments took place in the church. At Antioch some believers from Cyprus began to preach Christ to the Greeks, generally, and many believed and were added to the membership by way of baptism. This came to the ears of the apostolic leaders at Jerusalem, and they sent Barnabas to Antioch to investigate the matter. Barnabas was impressed by what he saw, affirmed the entry of the Gentiles into the faith, and took over the leadership of the church at Antioch. But he needed help, so he went to Tarsus, contacted Paul, and brought him back with him to become his assistant at Antioch. For the next year or so "they met with the church, and taught a large company of people; and in Antioch the disciples were for the first time called Christians" (Acts 11:26). This was now in the year A.D. 44 to 45.

The church at Jerusalem continued to be bothered by the question of admitting Gentiles into the faith, however. A serious controversy arose over some of Peter's actions. He had accepted an invitation to come down to Caesarea, to the house of a God-fearer by the name of Cornelius, a Roman centurion, to preach to a large company of Cornelius' family and friends. The decision was not an easy one for Peter, but he had had a vision, while in Joppa, which helped him decide (Acts 10:9 ff.). He had seen the heavens opening, and a large sheet full of all sorts of animals and reptiles and wild birds, let down by the four corners from heaven to earth. And there was a voice that said, "Rise, Peter; kill and eat." Peter had declared, "No, Lord; for I have never eaten anything that is common or unclean." But the voice persisted and said, "What God has cleansed, you must not call common." So, when the invitation from Cornelius came, Peter easily made the connection with his vision and accepted. His words, when he entered Cornelius' house, are revealing: "You yourselves know," he said, "how unlawful it is for a Jew to associate with or to visit anyone of another nation; but God has shown me that I should not call any man common or unclean" (v. 28). His sermon, likewise, is extraordinary:

"Truly [he said] I perceive that God shows no partiality, but in every nation any one who fears him and does what is right is acceptable to him. You know the word which he sent to Israel, preaching good news of peace by Jesus Christ (he is Lord of all), the word which was proclaimed throughout all Judea, beginning from Galilee after the baptism which John preached: how God anointed Jesus of Nazareth with the Holy Spirit and with power; how he went about doing good and healing all that were oppressed by the devil, for God was with him. And we are witnesses to all that he did both in the country of the Jews and in Jerusalem. They put him to death by hanging him on a tree; but

67

God raised him on the third day and made him manifest; not to all the people but to us who were chosen by God as witnesses. . . . And he commanded us to preach to the people, and to testify that he is the one ordained by God to be judge of the living and the dead. To him all the prophets bear witness that every one who believes in him receives forgiveness of sins through his name." (Acts 10:34-43)

Well, as Peter spoke, the story says, "the Holy Spirit fell on all who heard the word." Peter's companions, all circumcised Jews, were amazed at that—at the grace of God, seeing that the Holy Spirit was now given even to Gentiles." Then Peter declared, "Can any one forbid water for baptizing these people who have received the Holy Spirit just as we have?" So they were baptized.

When word got back to the brethren in Jerusalem that the Gentiles also had received the Word of God, Peter was called on the carpet and criticized by a group of Christian leaders described as "the circumcision party." "Why did you go to uncircumcised men?" they asked him. But Peter defended himself by telling of his vision, of the invitation, of what had happened at Cornelius' house. And he concluded: "If then God gave the same gift to them as he gave to us when we believed in the Lord Jesus Christ, who was I that I could withstand God?" (Acts 11:17). At that, the men of the circumcision party were silenced; they said, "Then to the Gentiles also God has granted repentance unto life."

But the struggle was not over. Barnabas and Paul had been sent out by the church at Antioch on their first missionary journey—this one to Cyprus and the southern part of Asia Minor (Turkey). They preached at many synagogues, and both Jews and Greeks were brought to faith. When they returned to Antioch, however, they found that a delegation had come from Jerusalem, teaching the brethren, "Unless you are circumcised according to the custom of Moses, you cannot be saved" (Acts 15:1). There arose what the Book of Acts describes as "no small dissension and debate," the outcome of which was that Paul and Barnabas were appointed to go to Jerusalem to iron out the question with the apostles and the elders.

This meeting, the so-called "first ecumenical council of the church" in A.D. 45, became the turning point in the history of Christianity. The issues to be decided had to do with the question of whether the Christian church was to remain a sect within Judaism or an open community of believers; whether the gospel of Christ was to be limited to Jews or be proclaimed to anyone who would hear it; whether Christ himself was to be considered the Jewish Messiah or be confessed as Lord and Saviour of all mankind. On the one hand were those who belonged to the circumcision party, saying, "It is necessary to circumcise them [the Gentiles], and to charge them to keep the law of Moses"—in other words, it is necessary to become a Jew before you can become a Christian. On the other hand were Peter, Paul, and Barnabas, arguing that God was already at work among the Gentiles, quite apart from circumcision and law. Peter's statement on this occasion was a gem of great clarity:

> "Brethren, you know that in the early days God made choice among you, that by my mouth the Gentiles should hear the word of the gospel and believe. And God who knows the heart bore witness to them, giving them the Holy Spirit just as he did to us; and he made no distinction between us and them, but cleansed their hearts by faith. Now therefore why do you make trial of God by putting a yoke upon the neck of the disciples which neither our fathers nor we have been able to bear? But we believe that we shall be saved through the grace of the Lord Jesus, just as they will." (Acts 15:7-11)

The ultimate outcome of the debate at Jerusalem was a decision in favor of openness—though the Judaizers, on James' suggestion, were able to include a charge that the Christians at Antioch "abstain from the pollutions of idols and from unchastity and from what is strangled, and from blood" (v. 20), all fundamental moral and dietary items considered most offensive to the Jewish mind. A letter outlining this ruling, and containing an endorsement of the ministry of Barnabas and Paul, was sent by special messengers to the church at Antioch. There it was received with much rejoicing. And soon Paul and Barnabas were sent off again, on separate missionary journeys this time. Paul's journey eventually took him to Greece, even to Athens, where he preached at the Areopagus and proclaimed the Christian message in close correlation with the idea of God contained in their own worship ("To an unknown god") and in the words of their own poets, "In him we live and move and have our being; . . . we are indeed his offspring" (Acts 17:28).

Let me include one additional historical note. The struggle with the Judaizers was never really over for Paul. In his Letter to the Galatians, which is largely an argument against the Judaizers, he tells the story of how he was forced to oppose Peter on the issue (Gal. 2:11 ff). It was in Antioch. Peter was visiting, and as long as he was there by himself, he went in and out among the Gentiles, eating with them as well. But as soon as certain people came down from Jerusalem, "he drew back and separated himself, fearing the circumcision party" (v. 12). To Paul, this was a sign of "insincerity"; Peter was "not straightforward about the truth of the gospel." So he told Peter off before them all:

"If you, a Jew, can live like a Gentile and not like a Jew, how can you demand that the Gentiles live like Jews? We who are Jews by birth and not Gentiles, but who know that a man is *not* justified by works of the law but through faith in Jesus Christ, even we have believed in Jesus Christ in order to be justified by faith. No one is justified by works of the law!" (Gal. 2:14-16, paraphrase)

The fact that Paul issued such an open and direct challenge to Peter's understanding of the gospel, not only orally before the church at Antioch, but in writing for all the churches all over Galatia to read, was a tremendous embarassment to Peter. He did manage to get even in the end, however. In the Second Epistle of Peter, the author puts in pen the following delightful slur:

Therefore, beloved, . . . be zealous to be found by him without spot or blemish, and at peace. And count the forbearance of our Lord as salvation. So also our beloved brother Paul wrote to you according to the wisdom given him, speaking of this as he does in all his letters. There are some things in them hard to understand, which the ignorant and unstable twist to their own destruction, as they do the other scriptures. You therefore, beloved, knowing this beforehand, beware lest you be carried away with the error of lawless men and lose your own stability. But grow in the grace and knowledge of our Lord and Savior Jesus Christ. (II Peter 3:14-18)

THE RADICAL INCLUSIVENESS OF THE GOSPEL

In the end it was the struggle with the Judaizers which came to put Paul in prison. He had just returned from his third missionary journey, and went directly to Jerusalem to report to James and the elders of the church. "He related one by one the things that God had done among the Gentiles through his ministry" (Acts 21:19). Then they told him of their concern:

"You see, brother, how many thousands there are among the Jews . . . who have believed; they are all zealous for the law, and they have been told about you that you teach all the Jews who are among the Gentiles . . . not to circumcise their children or observe the customs. What then is to be done? They will certainly hear that you have come." (Acts 21:20-22)

Then they suggested that Paul make an exhibition of his own obedience to the law. They had four men among them who were under a vow and would be going to the temple to purify themselves and make sacrifice, prior to shaving their heads. They urged Paul to go to the temple and purify himself along with them, perhaps even pay their expenses; "thus all will know that there is nothing in what they have been told about you but that you yourself live in observance of the law," they said. What was Paul to do? Any action of this nature would of course compromise his message of justification by faith, apart from the law. But could he refuse?

Some time earlier, Paul had written of himself:

Am I not free? Am I not an apostle? . . . For though I am free from all men, I have made myself a slave to all, that I might win the more. To the Jews I became as a Jew, in order to win Jews; to those under the law I became as one under the law—though not being myself under the law—that I might win those under the law. To those outside the law I became as one outside the law—not being without law toward God but under the law of Christ—that I might win those outside the law. To the weak I became weak, that I might win the weak. I have become all things to all men, that I might by all means save some. I do it all for the sake of the gospel. (I Cor. 9:1, 19-23)

So, Paul decided to go along with the suggestion—how could he do otherwise? He went with the men, purified himself, and entered the temple to notify the priests when the seven days would be fulfilled and the offering presented for the five of them. Before this process could be completed, however, some Jews from Asia recognized him, stirred up the crowd against him by shouting, "This is the man who is teaching men everywhere against the law and this place; he has defiled the temple." They almost succeeded in getting him killed, before soldiers of the Roman guard came on the scene and, mercifully, arrested him. Paul was never a free man again.

Now it is time we release ourselves from the historical perspective and bring the point of the story into some systematic order. I want to do that by way of a passage from the Letter to the Ephesians—a document definitely from the Pauline school, though probably not from Paul himself, since its Christology and ecclesiology are of a scope and character more representative of a later stage in the development of the early church. What we have here, we might say, is a mature expression of some distinctly Pauline elements of thought—the clearest reference I know of with regard to the radical extension of the commitment to Christ and the dramatic broadening of the scope of the gospel which the apostle Paul represents.

Here is the passage:

[I assume] that you have heard of the stewardship of God's grace that was given to me for you, how the mystery was made known to me by revelation, as I have written briefly. When you read this you can perceive my insight into the mystery of Christ, which was not made known to the sons of men in other generations as it has now been revealed to his holy apostles and prophets by the Spirit; that is, how the Gentiles are fellow heirs, members of the same body, and partakers of the promise in Christ Jesus through the gospel.

Of this gospel I was made a minister according to the gift of God's grace which was given me by the working of his power. To me, though I am the very least of all the saints, this grace was given, to preach to the Gentiles the unsearchable riches of Christ, and to make all men see what is the plan of the mystery hidden for ages in God who created all things; that through the church the manifold wisdom of God might now be made known to the principalities and powers in the heavenly places. This was according to the eternal purpose which he has realized in Christ Jesus our Lord, in whom we have boldness and confidence of access through our faith in him. (Eph. 3:2-12)

Let us include also this earlier statement:

Blessed be the God and Father of our Lord Jesus Christ, who has blessed us in Christ with every spiritual blessing in the heavenly places, even as he chose us in him before the foundation of the world, that we should be holy and blameless before him. He destined us in love to be his sons through Jesus Christ, according to the purpose of his will, to the praise of his glorious grace which he freely bestowed on us in the Beloved. In him we have redemption through his blood, the forgiveness of our trespasses, according to the riches of his grace which he lavished upon us. For he has made known to us in all wisdom and insight the mystery of his will, according to his purpose which he set forth in Christ as a plan for the fulness of time [namely], to unite all things in him, things in heaven and things on earth. (Eph. 1:3-10)

What a remarkable statement this is! What a vision!

I am hesitant even to try to reduce it to systematic propositions, but some attempt ought to be made to draw out the main points in some recognizable form. The awesome responsibility of this task is only alleviated by the awareness that in doing systematic theology this way, I am *not* trying to construct a system of thought of my own. I am simply listening to scripture and tradition, trying to understand what this deeper level of faith and commitment to Christ is all about. In this mood, I want to draw attention to the following main points:

1. *The newness of the revelation in Christ.* Paul (I am referring to Paul as the *authority* behind these statements, though not necessarily as the *author*) is speaking of a mystery which was not made known to earlier generations but which has now been revealed to the apostles and prophets in the church by the Holy Spirit. With this, several important things are said.

For one thing, there is the *clear recognition of progressive revelation.* Paul's statement is clearly directed to those who opposed the developments in the apostolic community on the grounds that both the message and the methods of the apostles constituted radical departures from the traditions of Judaism. In responding, Paul accepts the fact that the church appears to be inventing something new, but he claims that this newness is part of a larger process by which God makes his truth known to men. It is only from the point of view of an earlier, more limited revelation that the new seems to represent a departure from truth. Considered in the larger context of God's overall will and purpose, it can be seen simply as a new step in the progressive revelation of God's truth.

Second, in speaking of a mystery only now made known, Paul affirms that *although revelation is progressive, it is yet continuous.* In some translations, the word "mystery" is replaced by "secret." What is indicated here is that, although from *our* perspective that which is revealed appears to be new, from *God's* perspective it is not. It is something God had in mind all along, but which he only now has decided to make known. There is no difficulty in affirming that God may reveal *one* thing at *one* point and *something else* at *another*; the continuity of revelation does not have to be established along horizontal lines. The principle of continuity—that which ties together both what is revealed and what is still secret—is God's own eternal truth.

In the third place, Paul is quite unapologetic about his claim that the new revelation has only now been *given to the apostles and prophets in the church,* among whom—though he says he is the least—he clearly reckons himself. In making this claim, Paul is explicitly referring to the authority of the Holy Spirit as the foundation of apostleship; this is what puts *him* in the same order of apostleship as the original twelve. Moreover, he affirms that the growing edge of God's revelation has now been transferred from the people of the old order, the old covenant, to the people of the new order, the church of Christ. Paul is quite clear on this point: The church represents a new order; what it stands for is radically different from the old order. This fact does not leave the church rootless, however; Paul affirms that its roots are deep in the design of God, only now made clear through the revelation given the apostles by the inspiration or enlightenment of the Holy Spirit.

Fourth, we should note that the *new revelation, as it is described by Paul, focuses on Christ.* The mystery which only now is revealed is the mystery of Christ; the revelation which is given the apostles through the Holy Spirit is the revelation of Christ. The church, the new people of God, is the church of Christ; and the apostles, to whom the revelation is given, are "the apostles of Christ." Christ, for Paul, is the center and core of the new truth that has been revealed. It is the message *of* Christ and the commitment *to* Christ that set the church apart from everything that has gone before; and by the same token, it is the message of *Christ* and the commitment to *Christ* that put the church in the mainstream of that which is to come. Christ is the alpha and the omega, the beginning and the end of the church.

2. *The second main point in the Pauline statement in Ephesians has to do with God's eternal plan.* Paul speaks of an "eternal purpose" and "will," by which God, "who created all things . . ., chose us in [Christ] before the foundation of the world" and set forth "a plan for the fulness of time" which has now been "realized in Christ Jesus our Lord." This is where Paul begins to give *content* to the new revelation in Christ. He is beginning to explain what the mystery of Christ is all about, and in the process he develops what amounts to a full, systematic concept of God's relationship to the world and man, in christological terms.

Note what he is saying: First, that the *Christ-event was an integral part of God's design for the world from the beginning.* Far from being an emergency measure, instigated when God's original purposes were not fulfilled because of sin, and only when all other attempts to overcome the situation failed, Christ is declared positively purposed from the beginning, as the manifestation of God's eternal will and purpose. This, clearly, makes the message of Christ far more significant than anyone heretofore realized. The Christ-event can no longer be perceived as a last, desperate move on God's part—an extreme measure by which he tried to salvage what he could out of a world gone awry. On the contrary, before all things, before the world and men were even made, the relationship of God to the realities that he had in mind to bring forth had its focus in Christ. In short, all reality, all God's activity in history, everything God has ever done—it is all informed by a single purpose, a purpose formed in reference to Christ.

Note also that *Paul takes the Christ-event to be the realization of the plan which God had designed for the fullness of time.* Far from being the first step in a process which eventually would lead to the fulfillment of God's purposes—when sin would be overcome and men would live in righteousness and peace—Christ is taken to be the *actual* realization of the will and purpose of God among men. Here again is an affirmation which makes the message of Christ more meaningful than usually perceived. As Paul saw it, Christ could no longer be considered simply a means by which God made fulfillment *possible*, or a mediator through whom men learned that fulfillment was *feasible*; rather, Christ is to be taken as the active realization of God's will, the actual fulfillment of his plan and purpose. In a word, for Paul, what God did and does in Christ has once and for all established that state of affairs which God had in mind from the beginning.

This, on the surface, may seem like a strange idea. But Paul persists, speaking of "the unsearchable riches of Christ," through which we have been "blessed . . . in Christ with every spiritual blessing in the heavenly places . . . that we should be holy and blameless before him." What this refers to is of course the Pauline doctrine of justification. What must be noted in this connection is the emphasis that holiness and blamelessness before God is not a work of man, but of God; it is not a requirement or an accomplishment on our part but a blessing or a gift of God. Paul has learned that God, the righteous one, does not wait, passively, for man to achieve righteousness before he declares him justified, blameless before God. Quite the opposite is the case. God's righteousness is an active, justifying force. God himself is the justifying agent, not only *declaring* us justified before him, but also actually *making* us righteous by the working of his Spirit within and upon us.

3. *The third major point in the Ephesians passage is Paul's reference to predestination by love.* The reference to God's active justifying work, by which he fulfills his own purposes with us, is set in immediate correlation to the declaration of God's love as the sole motivation for the entire plan. Says Paul, "He destined us in love to be

his sons [and daughters] through Jesus Christ" and "chose us in him before the foundation of the world." The image drawn is that of a Father-Creator-Redeemer whose only thought, whatever he does, is to make expression of his own love, inclusively, unendingly, unqualifiedly, toward man.

This image is extraordinary, in several ways. It is clear, for example, that *Paul makes predestination coterminous with divine love.* There is no double predestination—one by love, the other by wrath; one *for* love, the other *for* wrath. God is love, and his love is behind all that he does, even his wrath. A single purpose, chosen out of his love from the beginning, directs all his works. God *created* us in love, the love in which he also *destined* us to be his children; and he *redeemed* us in love and thus made us his sons and daughters twice over. God's plan and purpose, for all his children, is that they be his children.

This means also that *all mankind is included in God's eternal plan.* There is a divine purpose in all human existence; wherever, however, whatever man is, he is destined for sonship. God, who in his love made us all, will not as Father love only some. His love is universal. His sons and daughters will not come from a single nation or a single race. God, who as Creator destined us all to live, will not as Redeemer destine only some to live fully. His love is not selective. Nor is it passive.

Not only does Paul make God's love the sole motivation for the eternal plan of creation and salvation; a *third* extraordinary feature at this point is *his view that Christ is the manifestation both of God's predestining and consummating love.* This makes *Christ the universal expression of God's will for man's sonship*; both by way of his role in the design and by way of his work in the world, he is the key figure in realization of God's eternal plan for all mankind. The important thing to be observed here is how Paul seems to have *widened* the consideration of Christ as mediator between God and man. No longer is he a figure who rises out of a particular nation or religious tradition, as a priest or a prophet or a king, challenging his people and turning them to righteousness, making them a new nation, a people of God, a light to all the world. Paul considers Christ a *mediator, not between man and God, but between God and man.* Christ, on this level of

Pauline thought—even Christ Jesus—is not so much a local or national figure who serves to bring a people to God; he is God's representative among men, and his life and work, his message and death, have significance as revelatory of God's grace toward all mankind. This is the tremendous scope of the Pauline vision of Christ.

4. *We focus next in the Ephesians passage on the Pauline doctrine of salvation by grace.* The passage we quoted speaks of grace, in no uncertain terms, as the primary expression of God's love. Paul's ministry is a "stewardship of . . . grace"; in fact, Paul says, he was made a minister "according to the gift of God's grace which was given me by the working of his power." God's great gift is the "glorious grace which he freely bestowed on us in the Beloved," in whom "we have redemption through his blood, the forgiveness of our trespasses, according to the riches of his grace which he lavished upon us." We are here, clearly, at the center of Pauline theology, and there are several important emphases to be noted.

First of all, there is the *consistent emphasis on the active, outgoing, dynamic quality of grace.* If Paul had been a Methodist, he would have used the term "prevenient" grace; he did not use the term, but he was clearly Methodist in doctrine! What we are talking about is the view that grace is not merely a friendly *disposition* on the part of God, a benign attitude with which he meets sinners when they repent and return to obedience; rather, God *manifests* his grace "preveniently"—before anything we do, whether repentance or faith. In Paul's view, grace is not passive and waiting. On the contrary, it is active, working. That is how he himself had experienced it.

The second emphasis we must note is *the inclusive, universal character of grace.* Grace is the dynamic expression of God's love, and since God's love is universal and inclusive, grace is equally so. There is no thought in Paul that grace is selective, or that it is restricted in any way, bottled up within holy vessels or administered only through certain channels. When he talks of his own "stewardship of . . . grace," he does not for a moment think that he is in control of it, or that grace is obtainable only through his ministry. God's grace is greater than that; it is grace *for* all, *in* all, through *Christ.*

A third characteristic emphasis here has to do with *the free, unqualified nature of grace, grace as "gift."* It is "freely bestowed on us in the Beloved" (which is Christ), "given me [he says] by the working of his power." There is no fear of "cheap grace" on the part of Paul—unless it would be that cheap grace still would be thought of as coming at a price. As he sees it, grace is free. It is *not* simply *offered*, set forth as a *possibility*, something we can obtain *if, when,* or *in so far* as we qualify; it is *given*, "bestowed," "lavished upon us." It is made manifest among men without any requirement or work of law. There is no timidity in Paul's mind with regard to the free gift of grace.

Then, fourth, we must note that Paul *takes redemption and forgiveness of sins to be an objective, once-for-all, universally significant event.* Through Christ, by way of his blood—that is, his utter self-giving—God has set forth a positive sign of his eternal love and grace. The redemptive work of Christ, as Paul sees it, is not merely a sign that God *will* save, that he *can* forgive, or that he *wishes* to redeem. The cross of Christ means, instead, that God *has* saved, forgiven, redeemed. It is an accomplished fact. Christ's work is the salvation of mankind, set forth, once and for all, in the middle of human history! It says, to all men and for all time, that God is love, that he relates to the world in grace, that *he is* reconciled, that atonement *is made*, that salvation *is accomplished*. What a message this is!

5. *The next major note in Paul's statement in Ephesians is the inclusiveness of the gospel.* We cannot talk about Paul's message without using the word "gospel." He himself uses that term. "Of this gospel I was made a minister," he says. But the term "this," "this gospel," points to the special character of Paul's message. He was aware that he had a particular task; that his message was of a peculiar nature. *His* task was "to preach to the Gentiles the unsearchable riches of Christ, and to make all men see what is the plan of the mystery hidden for ages in God who created all things." Once more we have this reference to "the mystery," the mystery of Christ, which was "not made known to the sons of men in other generations as it has now been revealed" to the apostles and prophets "by the Spirit." What is its content? What is the hidden plan of God? Here it is: "how the

Gentiles are fellow heirs, members of the same body, and partakers of the promise in Christ Jesus through the gospel."

The extraordinary thing about this, first of all, is that *Paul makes the covenant of God, with all that it stands for, as relevant to Gentiles, to the world at large, as it is to Jews, to the people of Israel.* With this he has taken the Christian gospel out of the context of Jewish exclusivism, out of the traditions of the old covenant, proclaiming it as the Word of God to the entire *ekumene*—the whole inhabited world. God is no longer simply the God of Israel, restricted in his covenanting mercy to the promises made to Abraham, Moses, and David. There is a greater covenant, namely, "the promise in Christ Jesus through the gospel," by which the Gentiles are made equal participants, "fellow heirs, members of the same body"—the body of Christ, which is the new, universal people of God.

How extraordinary Paul's gospel is becomes evident, when we observe *how the new people of God, the body of Christ, the church, takes on the inclusive character of the gospel.* Included, says Paul, are Jews and Greeks, rich and poor, high and low, wise and simple, East and West, slaves and free (and, had he lived today, hard-hats and long-hairs), men and women (he *did* include that)—*any* man and *any* woman who hears the gospel, accepts its message, and believes the Word of God in Christ. Here, all the differences among men are irrelevant—no walls of separation are left standing. To all the multitudes of the earth God has given the same promise: The promise of sonship, redemption, forgiveness of sins. God's eternal plan, determined as it was by his love, is that we should all be saved by his grace, through love.

There is a third extraordinary note here which we must not miss, namely, the fact that Paul *takes the new covenant, "the promise in Christ Jesus through the gospel," to be inclusive of all men without qualification.* The promise is given to sinners and righteous alike. What constitutes us as members of the Body of Christ is not some quality, some value, some standard or requisite in us; rather, in Christ, God has pronounced us to be his sons and daughters simply and solely on the basis of *his* love and grace. There is no other qualification required; there are no other prerequisites. God, in

Christ, has done all that is necessary; in him we can all "have boldness and confidence of access through our faith in him."

6. *Now, finally, the sixth major point in Paul's thought in this context—his reference to the ultimate goal.* The Ephesians passage closes with a stirring statement concerning the final purpose of God, his "plan for the fulness of time," namely, "to unite all things in [Christ], things in heaven and things on earth." "The fulness of time" *can* of course be taken to refer to the coming of Christ and the realization of God's eternal plan and purpose already accomplished in the Christ-event. The unity of all things in Christ would then refer to the church, in which all walls of separation have been removed. But "the fulness of time" *can also* be understood as an eschatological reference to the end of time or the second coming—the final phase of the Christ-event, when the Lordship of Christ shall be made manifest for all to see. The unity of all things, "things in heaven and things on earth," then speaks of a universal fulfillment, a final consummation of God's eternal plan and purpose, which is nothing less than perfection.

To be noted here is the daring proclamation *that God, who in his love sent everything forth in the beginning, will in the end gather everything in, in Christ.* This is how high and complete the Pauline commitment to Christ has become. For us, the doctrine of consummation has fallen apart under the impact of Greek and Persian dualism. We tend to think of the end in terms of final bifurcation of good and evil, a separation of the saved and the damned—and there are New Testament texts influenced by these traditions that will support such a view. But it is a view that assumes that God's plan has failed and that he finally gives up. That is not how Paul understands God. He sees Christ as the active love of God, involving himself in the situation of man, identifying himself with man, and humbling himself as man, so as to become one with us, even in sin—even so as to die the death of a sinner.

The earliest generations of Christian theologians at times referred to Christ as "descending into hell," there "preaching to the spirits in bondage." Medieval theologians developed the image of "the harrowing of hell" to express generally the same sentiment. In Pauline language, the idea that the redeeming work of Christ will ultimately be universally acknowledged is perhaps best expressed in the following words from the return cycle of the so-called "kenotic hymn":

Therefore God has highly exalted him and bestowed on him the name which is above every name, that at the name of Jesus every knee should bow, in heaven and on earth and under the earth, and every tongue confess that Jesus Christ is Lord, to the glory of God the Father. (Phil. 2:9-11)

That, I would suggest, is the very pinnacle of New Testament Christology. You can hardly reach a greater vision of Christ than that!

## CHAPTER 5

# The Universal Christ—
# Faith as Christocentric Universality

We have, to this point, considered three distinct stages in the early development of Christian faith, or as we have described them here, three levels of commitment to Christ: the disciples' confession that Jesus of Nazareth was the Christ; the emergence after the death of Jesus of the spiritual breakthrough at Pentecost; the radical expansion of the gospel of Christ in relation to the Gentile world, represented primarily in the ministry of the apostles Peter and Paul.

Our summary in the last chapter of the mature Pauline Christology that is set forth in the Epistle to the Ephesians has already given an image of the *fourth* stage or level of christological reflection evident in the New Testament: the level of universal Christocentricity or Christocentric universality.

Paul's reference to the mystery of Christ, the secret plan which God had in mind from the beginning, which was realized in Jesus Christ, and which is now proclaimed universally through the gospel, already suggests that the Christology of the early church was undergoing what we might describe as a vast systematic enlargement. *The Christ-event was now set into the context of the full history of salvation; it was, in fact, seen as the key to the understanding of all God's mighty works on behalf of man and the world, universally, from beginning to end.*

This meant, first of all, that the commitment to Christ as the center and core of truth, as the focal point of all God's dealings with things—all things—was radically intensified. It meant also that the interpretation of Christ as the active manifestation of God in the world, in the full scope of nature and history, creation and redemption, was vastly expanded. The Christ-event was extended, so to speak, far beyond the present manifestation of God in the person and work of Jesus of Nazareth, midstream in history, *backward* through the history of salvation, into prehistory, into the eternal counsel of God himself, and *forward* into the future, even to the final consummation, the fulfillment of God's eternal plan.

These developments came about by what we might desribe as a ripple-effect process.

At first there was only the historical figure of Jesus, the carpenter's son from Nazareth turned preacher after being baptized by John. Interpreting his own ministry in the light of the messianic symbols passed down through the prophetic-apocalyptic traditions of his people, he nurtured in his followers the conviction that the kingdom of God was here among them, and they responded with the confession that he was the Christ. That was the initial stage of Christian faith—the pebble was dropped, and as it hit the water, the first ripple appeared. Jesus of Nazareth was believed to be the Christ of God. We are at the Markan, the eyewitness, the "Caesarea-Philippi" stage of faith.

Then Jesus was crucified—the pebble disappeared. But as it sank into the water, wider, more powerful ripples were stirred. Faith now came to encompass not only the "facts," the ministry and teachings of Jesus; it included the significance of his life in the salvation history of the world, the meaning of his birth and death, as well. His death was interpreted as atonement, his birth as the fulfillment of messianic prophecies. Jesus of Nazareth was believed to be the redeemer promised out of the house of David, the suffering servant prophesied by Isaiah. The Synoptic Gospels, with their genealogies and passion narratives, are the symbols of this stage.

The next ripple, more powerful yet, followed quickly. Faith, stirred to the conviction that Jesus' coming and end were both within the transcendent purposes of God, could no longer consider his birth his beginnings or his death his end. The son of Joseph was now interpreted to be the Son of God, born of a woman but not of flesh; and the crucified Jesus was now confessed to be the living Lord, raised by God and alive in the Spirit. We are at the stage where Christology became synonymous with the symbols of virgin birth and resurrection.

Then we see the circles of the ripples become larger and larger, deeper and more powerful, as the force of the faith grew stronger. The open confession that Jesus was the Son of God soon gave rise to the conviction that he had come to earth out of heavenly preexistence; and the forceful proclamation of the resurrection faith quickly gave impetus to the conviction that he was now, once again, "at the right hand of the Father." We are at the stage of the so-called Logos-Christology—Christ being seen, in Johannine language, as the "Word" which was with God in the beginning and which became flesh, and at the other end of the spectrum, as the ascended and exalted Lord, now active as our heavenly high priest in the presence of the Almighty. The ripples have now become strong waves; the circles of faith are almost as wide as the ocean. Yet the force and the circumference of faith seem only to continue to increase.

One final, more powerful dimension yet came to be added to New Testament Christology: the conviction, on the one hand, that the preexistent Christ, the Logos of God, had not only been *with* God in the beginning, but that he *was* God—God of God, equal with God, of the substance and nature of God—and the vision, on the other hand, that the ascended and exalted Christ, now "at the right hand of the Father," is not only the *mediator* between God and man, but is himself *the sovereign Lord of the universe*—"the king in the kingdom of God," "the name above every name," the one in whose name "every knee should bow, in heaven and on earth and under the earth, and every tongue confess that Jesus Christ is Lord, to the glory of God the Father" (Phil. 2:10-11). We are at the beginning stage of *christological metaphysics*, with theologians speaking in the presumptuous imagination of poets and philosophers of the transcendent nature and essence of Christ, and of *eschatological universalism*, with seers celebrating in the foreshortened perspective of patriarchs and prophets the Christ who is the alpha and the omega, the beginning and the end, the first and the last, the all in all.

With this, the faith that started out as a faint ripple on the Sea of Galilee has risen into a mighty flood wave that fills the entire universe.

The commitment to Christ, which began in respone to the simple question, "Who do you say that I am?" has now matured into a universal Christology, proclaimed in terms of Christocentric universality. The scope and sweep of this faith-commitment is nothing less than astounding. The structure and content of the Christology that came out of it is no less impressive; it is rich, in depth and height, in thought as well as feeling.

Listen to some of the hymns and prayers and benedictions from the early church that have been included at various points in the New Testament writings. We have already referred to the so-called "kenotic hymn" in Philippians 2. Here are some other examples:

He [God] has delivered us from the dominion of darkness and transferred us to the kingdom of his beloved Son, in whom we have redemption, the forgiveness of sins.

He [Christ] is the image of the invisible God, the first-born of all creation; for in him all things were created, in heaven and on earth, visible and invisible, whether thrones or dominions or principalities or authorities—all things were created through him and for him. He is before all things, and in him all things hold together. He is the head of the body, the church; he is the beginning, the first-born from the dead, that in everything he might be pre-eminent. For in him all the fulness of God was pleased to dwell, and through him to reconcile to himself all things, whether on earth or in heaven, making peace by the blood of his cross. (Col. 1:13-20)

For Christ also died for sins once for all, the righteous for the unrighteous, that he might bring us to God, being put to death in the flesh but made alive in the spirit; in which he went and preached to the spirits in prison, who formerly did not obey, when God's patience waited. . . . [He] now saves you, . . . through the resurrection of Jesus Christ, who has gone into heaven and is at the right hand of God, with angels, authorities, and powers subject to him. (I Pet. 3:18-22)

Great indeed, we confess, is the mystery of our religion:
> He was manifested in the flesh,
> vindicated in the Spirit,
>   seen by angels,
> preached among the nations,
> believed on in the world,
>   taken up in glory. (I Tim. 3:16)

## FAITH AS CHRISTOCENTRIC UNIVERSALITY

In many and varied ways God spoke of old to our fathers by the prophets; but in these last days he has spoken to us by a Son, whom he appointed the heir of all things, through whom also he created the world. He reflects the glory of God and bears the very stamp of his nature, upholding the universe by his word of power. When he made purification for sins, he sat down at the right hand of the Majesty on high, having become as much superior to angels as the name he has obtained is more excellent than theirs. (Heb. 1:1-4)

Now, before going any further, let me make three or four points that have importance for our understanding of New Testament Christology as a whole.

First, the *Christology which we see developed in the New Testament and expressed in such stirring language must be understood for what it is: as the expression of a faith-commitment.* This means that the *content* of Christology is *itself* commitmental, not merely that the subjective appropriation or response to it is.

It is important that we come to understand this. At times when we talk about the Christian commitment we consider it simply the subjective side of a subject-object relationship. Out there is the object, the fact of Christ, perfectly capable of standing by itself. As an object, Christ is not affected by our faith; whether or not men believe in him does not make any difference as to the reality of who or what he is. What happens when a person believes is simply that he makes a personal commitment to the Christ as Christ and affirms that the objective Christ is now perceived *by him*, the believer, to be what he is *in himself*, the Christ.

I shall not, in this context, undertake to critique this viewpoint or answer the epistemology that underlies it, except to say that it is clearly based on the questionable assumption of a separation or dichotomy—over-againstness—of subject and object, the knower and the known. In commonsense contexts—where we deal with things—this assumption works pretty well. But religion is not commonsense; faith is not like empirical knowledge. Faith is *confronted by objects*; but the *approach faith takes to these objects* is not simply the acknowledgment of the objective qualities of the objects as objects. Faith represents rather *a subjective interpretation of these objects as the believer perceives them*—i.e., as faith interprets them.

Thus, the Christology of the New Testament is not simply the presentation of an objective, historical-empirical, or metaphysical-theoretical fact, in response to which the writers subsequently express their personal faith-commitment, saying that this factual truth is also held to be true by them. Rather, *the New Testament's Christology is a series of testimonies to the meaning that believers see in Jesus of Nazareth, and from the perspective that they see him.* As Hans Küng puts it, the New Testament sources are "*committed testimonies of faith meant to commit their readers:* documents not by non-participants but by convinced believers wanting to appeal for faith in Jesus Christ and which therefore take the form of an interpretation or even a profession of faith."[1]

Second, let me suggest that *the language in which the Christology of the New Testament is set forth must be understood as it is intended: as the imaginative symbolism through which faith expresses itself.* Once more we are saying that the *content* of Christology is itself symbolic, not merely that the style and terminology are.

We must make sure we take note of this point. On occasion, when we talk about symbols, myths, and metaphors, we give the impression that these are all matters of style. Scratch the surface of the symbol and there is the solid fact; look into the marrow of the myth and there is transcendent reality; follow the metaphor to its meaning and there is being. We say, with Tillich, "Symbols participate in that which they symbolize," or with the form critics, "Myths are stories from this side concerned with things on the other side."

It is not my purpose to engage in polemics, but I must emphasize that the symbolic nature of the New Testament symbols—even the mythological character of New Testament myths—must be acknowledged and respected. To claim that they are somehow *representative of transcendent things* is to make them into metaphysical-theoretical signs; they are then meaningful only to the extent that they can be proven to represent these transcendent things truly—i.e., they become subject to verification and falsification. And since the New Testament language obviously claims to represent something which is otherwise unknown and unknowable, it falls under the criticism of commonsense as nonsense.

No, we must acknowledge that the christological symbols and theological myths that are set forth in the New Testament are not of the order of referential language; rather they are of the character of expressive language. The meaningfulness of this kind of language does not lie in what it refers *to*, but what it derives *from*. And what the christological symbols and myths derive *from* is precisely Christian faith—i.e., the commitment to Jesus as the Christ and the faithful interpretation of his life and work. This does not weaken the meaning of the christological language; there is no reason to say that Christology is *mere* myth or *just* symbol. Myths are true when they truly express the meaning of the faith; symbols are meaningful when they make meaningful witness to the faith-commitment in which they originate.

When this is said, a third point must also be made, namely, that *the Christology of the New Testament must be understood in the light of its character: as a varied, multifaceted, evolving witness to a developing commitment to Christ.* This is to say that Christology is itself a process of Christocentric theological reflection; that it is dynamic, not static; that it is developing, not given; and that it is open-ended, not closed.

We cannot emphasize this point enough. When we talk about New Testament Christology, we often think of it as a completed system, a consistent structure, a finished doctrine. Everything fits in; every part goes with every other part. After all, we say, the New Testament is the ultimate revelation of God; it would not be reasonable to think that God says something to one person, and something else to another. Christology is the center and core of Scripture; it must be logically consistent, systematically one.

Once again I must resist the urge to be critical—I am myself, a systematic theologian. But I must confess my uneasiness at the tendency of systematic theologians to impose their own kind of *systematics* on that which is merely *systemic,* or their propensity to take as *metaphysical* and *theoretical* that which is clearly *metaphorical* and *symbolic.*

We must resist these tendencies. New Testament Christology will lose both its historical and its theological character if it is reduced to theoretical dogma; its dynamic qualities will disappear if it is pressed into static doctrinal formulas. There is no single christological orthodoxy in the New Testament; there are several, on different levels, and expressing different stages of faith.

Fourth, this means that *the New Testament's Christology must be interpreted relative to where it is: at the formative stages of Christian faith and doctrine.* This gives tremendous significance to the New Testament's witness to Christ; but it means also that we recognize the historical relativity of this witness.

This point must not be ignored. When we approach the message of the New Testament we often forget that it was first proclaimed *to,* believed *by,* and spread *through* human beings. We tend to think of revelation as having come directly from heaven, untouched by human minds—pure and absolute in form as well as in content. But this is altogether unrealistic; it is also quite unbiblical. If there is anything that is typical of the biblical view of revelation, it is that it is historical, located in time and place, and developing *through* time and *in relation to* place. God's Word is spoken through men; even when the Word of God comes in its purest form, it comes incarnate—as the Word made flesh.

We acknowledge and affirm, then, the historicity—the historical relativity—of New Testament Christology. It emerged at first among men who thought in the thought-forms of the Hebrew people, formed their concepts under the influence of post-exilic, apocalyptic Judaism, and spoke in the common language of Palestine at the time, namely, Aramaic. It was then transplanted among people of a Hellenistic, Greek background, people whose thought-forms, concepts, and language were informed by developments in the dominant culture at the time—the continuing influence of Platonism, the impact of Greek mystery religions, and the characteristics of the popular language of the area, *koine* Greek. Later, as the church spread throughout the Roman Empire, Roman and Latin culture superseded the Hebrew and Greek influence of the early years; Roman thought-forms, concepts, and symbols came to be formative for christological reflection.

We see evidence of this historicity, this relativity to culture, within the New Testament as well as in the Christology of the post-biblical period. Christian faith-reflection did not take place in a vacuum; neither was it allowed to be locked into a single set of thought-forms or concepts, or limited to a certain language or vocabulary. It "incarnated" itself again and again, finding new forms within each cultural context where the Christian message found receptivity and where the faith came alive.

With this as background, let us now return to the ripple analogy and the four distinct stages in the development of Christology which we have found evident in the New Testament. We can now affirm *that each of these stages, each of these expanding waves of faith-reflection, emerged in response to certain definite conditions in the historical situation of these believers.*

Let me summarize these quickly. The first disciples were part of a social and political situation that threatened the very existence of Jewish culture and Jewish religion. In this situation, many preachers and prophets came on the scene, some proclaiming themselves to be the Messiah, others as forerunners of the Anointed One. The apocalyptic hopes and expectations of the Jewish people were running high. In this situation the disciples were faced with the challenge to follow one particular man, Jesus of Nazareth, and to believe his preaching that the kingdom God had promised to establish was actually here, that it was to be ruled by his own representative, the Son of man, and that Jesus was that Son of man, God's Christ. It was in the crucible of this challenge that the first Christian confession, "Jesus is Christ," was formed.

At the death of Jesus this historical situation of the believers changed. He was no longer among them. His own people, the chosen people of God, had rejected and killed him. That seemed to be the end of his message—the religious and political establishment had crushed him. The challenge these early Christian believers now faced was: Could they continue to believe Jesus, even when they could no longer observe him? Could they still confess him to be the Christ, even though he had suffered ignominious death? Their faith not only survived the challenge; it came out strengthened. Their memory was

91

filled with the recollection of his message, and their spirits with an overwhelming sense of his continuing Presence among them. They came out of that situation with a new Christian confession: "Jesus Christ is risen!"

Then the church's situation changed again. While the Jewish community generally continued to reject the message of Christ, the apostles found a hearing among the Gentiles. With this, they were faced with yet another crucial challenge: Should they preach the Christ as the Jewish Messiah and incorporate in the church only those who were Jews, or who first converted to Judaism, or should they accept the gospel's progress in the world as a sign that God had already made the new covenant to include the Gentiles and encompass the whole world? Should Christianity remain a sect within Judaism, or should it venture forth on its own and raise up for God a new people out of the tribes and nations of the earth? The decision, as we have seen, was for the radical openness of the gospel. Once again the Christian confession was enlarged; Christians now proclaimed Jesus Christ "the Savior of the world."

With the expansion of the Christian mission to the Gentile world, still another major adjustment in christological thought and language was forced upon the early church. The gospel of Christ now had to be enlarged so as to encompass all of history and the whole world; moreover, it had to be expressed in such a way as to be understandable and acceptable to the Greek and Roman mind. The challenge at this point was not only to find a way to relate the particularity of the Jewish Jesus to the universality of divine being, but also to conceptualize the Christ in the thought-forms and categories of Greek and Roman culture itself. It was out of this situation that the Logos-Christology and the "kenotic" patterning of the Christian kerygma developed. Christ was now presented as "the essence and core of the divine being," as the "eternal Word," of the same "nature" and "substance" as God, and as the historical "incarnation" of the divine will to salvation, the universal "emanation" of divine love and power.

We could continue this story. Within the New Testament itself, and beyond it, in the theology of the early church fathers, other such developments took place—further expansions of christological reflection and interpretation emerging in response to constantly changing situations. We could mention the adjustments that resulted from historical events such as the fall of Jerusalem, or from religious developments such as the delay of the *parousia*. These situations caused the Christian community to give increased emphasis to the concept of the Second Coming and at the same time push this final phase of the Christ-event far into a distant and unknown future. And we could point to certain internal ecclesiastical developments such as the threat of heresy in the church—situations that gave rise not only to an increased emphasis on apostolic succession, spiritual authority being passed down by the laying on of hands from those who were first chosen by Christ himself, but which brought to the forefront of the believers' lives the sacraments, creeds, and canons of the church as the official and normative channels through which the true teaching and real Presence of Christ continuously were made manifest in the world.

The point I wish to make is this: If we observe and consider valid the process through which Christology developed *within* New Testament Christianity, or *during* the apostolic period, we cannot reasonably disregard or consider invalid the process of christological enlargement and adjustment which took place in the church *following* the apostolic era. One cannot logically argue that such developments are to be accepted within the New Testament itself but that further expansions of Christology, after the close of the New Testament canon, or today, must be deemed inappropriate or unnecessary. Neither history nor thought has been made to stand still following the establishment of the biblical canon or after the formulation of the early creeds. New situations, new problems, and new perspectives have continued to develop. Clearly, the christological reflection of those who continue to be committed to Christ must be allowed to develop as well.

What I am suggesting, in short, is that the Christian faith-commitment must never be locked into static, dogmatic, once-for-all christological categories. The Christocentric faith-commitment has given rise to dramatically new and radically different dimensions of christological reflection at various points in the past; there is no reason to think that Christian believers cannot similarly be inspired in the present and in the future. We must conclude, in fact, that if *we* are to be as faithful to Christ in *our* time as earlier generations of Christians were in their day, we must continue to do in relation to *our* situation what they did in relation to theirs, namely, continue to expand our christological reflection in the light of, and in interaction with, the understanding of things that is characteristic of our time, our situation, and our culture. For those who are committed to Christ, Christology—Chritocentric theological reflection—is a never-ending task.

This brings me to the challenge before us in the final phases of the twentieth century—our task as Christian believers in the present age—which is to relate our Christology to a radically expanded understanding of the world.

No enlightened person living in the last third of the twentieth century can miss the significance of the new world picture that has developed in the space age. Though primarily a result of science and technology, it carries importance for every field of thought and every area of life, including religion.

The symbol-above-all-symbols of this new perspective on things is the picture of the planet earth, shrouded in clouds, suspended in space, framed by the blue-black expanse of the universe—a picture sent back to earth from a spacecraft that for a period of time had been thrown clear of the earth's gravitational sphere and was traveling to the moon with only an electronic link to home. That picture, shot from one spacecraft and picturing another, represented the first complete self-portrait of the earth. Earlier representations had been partial, limited by some horizon or by the picture's edge, or they had been fictitious, like a flat earth map or a colorful mounted globe. Now, clearer than ever before, we saw the earth as it really is, single and complete, whole and limited.

That picture of spaceship earth, the home of humanity, is a most potent reminder of certain basic facts about the world, about life, and about man—facts so fundamental as to be prior to any ideology, precedent to all social and political theory, preliminary to all systems of value and meaning. It presents us with such an elementary vision of reality as to call into question every philosophy, every viewpoint, every theory or action, whether individual or systematic, that is in any way partial or partisan, provincial or exclusive. It becomes, in fact, a basic criterion by which all our systems are judged, all our ideologies are tested, all our values evaluated, and all our actions scrutinized. It takes humanity in the direction of a completely new understanding of things, of new truth and new value, based on the most self-evident and universal a priori of all, the visible ground of our being: the earth. In providing us this total, holistic, inclusive view—the global view—this picture suggests that the time is ripe for a new revolution, for a breakthrough to radically different ways of thinking and acting. It becomes, in a sense, the logogram of a new age—*the global age, the age of the one earth, the age of humanity.*

In the area of religion, the new age forces us to raise a new question—or to face an old question in a new way—namely, *the relationship between Christianity and the other religions of the world or between Christocentric theological reflection and religious pluralism.* In the past, the Christian church has often expressed its Christocentric commitment in absolutist and exclusivistic ways. We have proclaimed Christ as "the one and only mediator between God and man" and the name of Jesus as "the only name given under heaven by which men may be saved." We have confronted devotees of other religions with the direct demand that they recognize Christ, otherwise they have no truth or value, and with the claim that only if they become Christians will they be acceptable to God on God's own terms. Such doctrines have caused great consternation, understandably, in these other religious communities; they have caused some unhappy side effects in Christian theology as well.

Think, for example, of the confusion caused by proclaiming that there is only one God, one Creator of all things, one Father of all men, and then declaring that this God has revealed himself only in the Bible or that salvation is brought about only in Jesus Christ. The consequence, inevitably, is a narrowing of the scope of revelation and an absolutization of the particular Christian view of salvation to such an extent that one can no longer consider any other religion related to God or God related to any other religion. This affects not only one's view of other religions, but also, more fundamentally yet, one's view of God as God. One actually says that God is particular, not universal, and that his work in the world is exclusive, not inclusive. One even suggests that there is a discrepancy between God's creative work and his redemptive work, or between his love and his grace.

In one sense we can say that the challenge which we face in the global age is similar to that which the early church faced in its relations to the Gentile world. In *their* case, the question was whether Christ should continue to be considered simply as the Jewish Messiah and whether those who believed in him had to become Jews before they became Christians. In *our* case, one might well say the correlative question is whether Christ is to be preached simply as the Christian Christ and whether everyone who is to be considered related to him must first become Christians. We have seen how the early apostles struggled over *their* question, finally reaching the decision that although Jesus of Nazareth was a Jew, and although they themselves were Jews, the spirit of Christ—faith in Christ—could not be restricted within the bounds of Judaism. *We* are now faced with a similar struggle; will we reach the correlative decision that although Christ is the focal point of Christian faith, and although we ourselves are Christians, the spirit of Christ—faith in Christ—cannot be restricted within the bounds of Christianity?

It is obvious that before we can reach that decision a certain expansion of Christology in the direction of universality similar to that which Paul originated in the early church needs to take place among us—an enlargement of the Christian kerygma to tie Christ into the universal plan of God for creation or to relate the special revelation in Christ to the general revelation in the world religions. Many theologians are looking seriously at this possibility. There is much talk of "anonymous Christians," "Christ incognito in the world religions," and other such suggestive phrases. But we have not come far in this direction. In fact, so far the theological effort can be criticized, to use Hans Küng's terminology, for sweeping "the whole of good-willed humanity . . . with an elegant gesture across the paper-thin bridge of a theological fabrication into the back door of the 'holy Roman Church,' " and for not facing the real challenge, namely, to have enough respect for the other faiths to declare that they are in fact valid faiths and that there is indeed salvation outside the Christian church. [2]

I shall not take this matter to its conclusion here. It is interesting, however, to observe that once again Paul was on the growing edge of things, far ahead of his time. We would do well to listen to him on this question as in so many other contexts. I am referring to his speech at Areopagus in Athens, summarized in Acts 17. Let me close this chapter by drawing out four important points from what Paul said on that occasion.

First, we notice that Paul complimented the Athenians for being "very religious." They had surrounded themselves with temples, shrines, altars, images—objects of worship of every description. They had an expressed interest in religious subjects and religious teachings—they liked to spend their time telling and hearing the latest new thing. They had in fact urged Paul to come up to their holy hill to make a formal presentation of his message. Paul was very impressed, and he opened his speech by pointing to the positive values in their religious orientation.

We have something to learn from this. We tend to disparage all such religiosity. We often declare that there is an absolute division—a complete separation—between Christianity and the other religions, as though Christianity is *not* a religion, or as though it is the *only* religion. Paul handled the matter differently; he established a point of contact with his hearers by emphasizing the *continuity* between the gospel he had come to preach and the religion they already held.

Second, we find Paul pointing to the basic *similarity* between their religion and the message he had come to bring. He had found an altar inscribed "To an unknown God," and said, "That which you worship, then, even though you do not know it, is what I now proclaim to you"—God "who gives life and breath and everything else to everyone," who "created" and formed them into different races to live over the earth, and who set limits to their times and spaces, "so that they would look for him, and perhaps find him as they felt around for him." Paul even quoted with approbation one of the Greek poets, who said, "In him we live and move and exist. . . . We too are his children" (Acts 17:23, 25, 27-28, TEV).

Once more we have something to learn. We often think of the other religions as having no relationship to God, and of other believers as being outside the family of God. It is a result of de-emphasizing the objective, "theocentric" doctrines of creation and redemption, and their correlative, the concept of a once-born, "natural" or "adopted" child of God, and focusing solely on the subjective, "anthropocentric" doctrines of sin and salvation, and their correlative, the concept of a twice-born, "born again" child of God. For Paul, clearly, there is only one God, and he is not far away from anybody; he is the Creator and Redeemer of all men. Known or unknown, God is the same God for all.

Third, Paul called attention to a fundamental truth that confronts men, all men, of whatever faith, in relation to God. He had noticed the multitude of idols the Athenians had produced—the images and structures that served to assure them of the presence of the divine in their midst. And he said, "God, who made the world and everything in it, is Lord of heaven and earth, and does not live in temples made by men. Nor does he need anything that men can supply by working for him, since it is he who gives life and breath and everything else to all men" (Acts 17:24-25, TEV). So, he said, "Since we are God's children, we should not suppose that his nature is anything like an image of gold or silver or stone, shaped by the art and skill of man" (Acts 17:29, TEV).

Again there is something we need to learn here. Paul spoke of idolatry in first person plural—"we." We most often speak of it in second or third persons plural—"you," "they." We seem to think that what is wrong with idols is that they are not *Christian* images or what is wrong with temples is that they are not churches—as though it is perfectly all right to think that God lives in our Christian temples or that he is really and truly represented by our Christian images. Paul does not allow such exceptions to the truth: God, he says, does not need any of our temples; the universe is his temple! He does not need anything we produce or contribute, whether gifts or work; he is the one who *gives* all things and works his own will *in* all things!

Finally, let us note that Paul ended his Areopagus speech with a clear word about Christ's place in God's universal design. He said, "God has overlooked the times when people did not know him, but now he commands all of them everywhere to turn away from their evil ways. For he has fixed a day in which he will judge the whole world with justice by means of a man he has chosen. He has given proof of this to everyone by raising that man from death!" (Acts 17:30-31, TEV). Notice that Paul makes Christ's role relevant to all men everywhere, to the whole world—to the judgment or redemption of everyone and everything, universally.

We must make sure that we understand this point. We often talk as though Christ is related exclusively to Christians or as though what God *has* done, *is* doing, and *will* do in the world is somehow restricted to the church or channeled solely through the church to the world. Paul doesn't see it this way; he sees Christ as loose in the world, active everywhere, among men of every faith, every race, every creed, every nation—among Jews and Gentiles, *in* the church and *beyond* it. In short, for Paul Christ is the manifestation of God's redemptive will and purpose, in every context and in all things, universally.

That is Christocentric universality or universal Christocentricity in a nutshell.[3]

Yet even this does not complete the christological picture or meet all the challenges before the Christian community of the present. Our situation not only confronts us with a global view of man and earth, forcing us to reconsider the question of the relationship between Christianity and other world religions; it brings us face to face with a startlingly new understanding of the world itself—of the universe, the cosmos, the nature of reality—thus forcing us to undertake still further attempts at expanding our Christology.

We shall pick up on that part of the story next.

## CHAPTER 6

Christ and the Expanding Universe

On July 20, 1976, a new era in the history of science was inaugurated. On that day, on the surface of the planet Mars, an American spacecraft—a miniature laboratory built by American engineers and sent aloft from Cape Kennedy some eleven months earlier—settled down after a perfect landing, having traveled approximately a quarter of a million miles from earth before entering an orbit around Mars and finally coming in for a soft landing on the Martian soil.

The Russians had landed a spacecraft on Venus, our closest neighbor in the solar system, the year before, but its capacities had been limited. Only now, with the landing of a compact space laboratory on Mars, was science actually taking steps to collect and analyze substances that could provide reliable answers to the question, Does life in any recognizable form exist elsewhere in our solar system?

The landing of Viking I came seven years to the day after the first visit of man to the moon. That earlier landing—when two men for the first time in history set foot on another body in space—had been an exciting event, signifying the maturation of man's capacity to travel through space, land, explore, and return home safely with a load of hard evidence with which to dispel the superstition and lift the ignorance of earlier generations. But the visits to the moon were still only backyard safaris compared with the exploration of Mars. The moon after all is the earth's moon, orbiting within the gravitational pull of the earth, and scientists already knew enough about it not to expect any signs of life there. With the landing on Mars, something infinitely more important was taking place. For the first time ever, experimental science was reaching out beyond the solar orbit of the earth, jumping so to speak across a vast chasm of space, to a planet that circles the sun in a different orbit from our own—and one which from all indications, could contain at least a semblance of the conditions considered prerequisite for life. Once there, Viking I, obedient to its orders, unfolded itself and began to scan the surroundings with its television eyes, scoop up soil with its remote control hands, analyze the samples with its computer brain, and send back to earth the resulting data with its telemetry voice.

What a magnificent enterprise it was—to that moment undoubtedly the crowning event in man's quest for knowedge, and for our time the most impressive proof of man's scientific and technological skills. Viking I may in fact have inaugurated a new era in human history.

It has not yet been determined whether Mars contains—or has contained—life. Chemical processes have been found which simulate those resulting from organic life on earth. In addition, evidence has been found of a shifting climate, of the presence of large areas of ice, and thus of the basic element of life, water. But whether anything there resembles the biological spheres of life on earth remains to be seen. A second Viking laboratory made a landing in another, more fertile region of the planet within a few weeks of Viking I. And recently even more sophisticated probes have been made to other planets in the solar system—to Jupiter, Saturn, and Uranus, billions of miles out. We shall soon know the answers to a number of questions men have only been able to speculate about up to now—answers we could not even have invented by imagination.

All of which boggles the mind. The developments we observe, and the period we are living through, are nothing short of revolutionary. For most of us, I am sure, these last few years have been filled with strange ideas and fantastic new perspectives. What if there is life elsewhere in the universe? What if in this third century of our nation's history, in this sixth millennium of recorded history on earth, we should suddenly discover that the earth is not unique, that in our own solar system, or beyond, are other planets resembling the earth at one stage or other in its development, and that intelligent beings have emerged elsewhere in the universe, just as man has here? What if we should finally find proof that the universe is populated by beings altogether different from ourselves, developed according to the natural conditions on their own planets, and according to the ages and eras of their own place in the cosmos?

Questions such as these have until recently been the playthings of science-fiction writers and visionaries—people whose imagination has made premature excursions into realms considered unknowable and unverifiable by most of us. But in the meantime, over the last century or so, scientists have developed both the methods and the means for *exploring* the universe—instead of just speculating about it. And as a result of the work of modern astronomers, astrophysicists, astrochemists, and most recently astrobiologists, an entirely new cosmology has been developed—one that cannot be ignored, the way the imaginations of philosphers and the machinations of science-fiction writers could in the past. It affects, in fact, every facet of our understanding of the world, from the dating of the earth's origins and the mapping of its place in the universe, to our concepts of the shape and size of the universe, the nature of life, and—ultimately—the origins of all things.

These developments that we face in the era symbolized by Viking I will undoubtedly come to affect our thinking fully as dramatically as did two earlier revolutions in the mind-set of Western man: *Copernicus' discovery* in the sixteenth century that the earth is not the center of the universe, but is one of several bodies that rotate around the sun; and *Charles Darwin's investigations* in the nineteenth century as to the origin of the species, proving man himself to be tied in with the natural processes of biological evolution on earth. If these earlier advancements in the knowledge of the world caused revoutionary changes in the way people understood things, Viking I and the scientific explorations of the universe which it symbolizes will have no less serious effects on us. So far, the description of our time as "the space age" has had reference primarily to certain technological advancements—the capacity of scientists and engineers to facilitate space travel and exploration. From now on, all the rest of us will be challenged to come to terms with the new picture of the world which is now developing, and this means not only updating our cosmology, our understanding of the world, but also bringing up-to-date our philosophy and theology as well.

Think of it for a minute. Forty-some years ago, when I started third grade in elementary school, even the most learned astronomers believed that the whole universe was made up of the stars and planets which we now ascribe to a single galaxy, the galaxy of the Milky Way. What we called the Milky Way back then has since turned out to be no more than a collection of stars in another portion of our galaxy—a particularly bright neighborhood in our galaxy, if you will. When I grew up, the earth was one of seven planets orbiting the sun—since then two more have been found—and the sun was considered unique among the stars, being the center of its own solar system.

Since then, astronomers have developed new and more powerful telescopes, optical and electronic, by which they can not only observe the stars and photograph them closely, but measure distances and movements in the universe as well—objects billions of light-years away (and a light-year, we should remember, is defined as the distance light travels, at the speed of 186,000 miles per second, in a year).

By way of these investigations, we now know that the Milky Way, our own immediate neighborhood in space, contains approximately one hundred billion stars or suns, many of which—scientists say one in one hundred—are surrounded by numbers of planets and thus form their own solar systems. Beyond this one galaxy there are as many additional galaxies as there are stars in the Milky Way—one hundred billion galaxies—each with its own billions of stars. Moreover, each of the galaxies can be observed to rotate in space—our own sun, for example, being located somewhat off-center in the Milky Way, will make one complete turn around the galaxy's center each two hundred million years. At the outskirts of each galaxy, in the gaseous, dusty trains they pull along, new stars apparently continue to be born. More extraordinary yet, scientists now know that the galaxies are all rushing outward, away from one another, as though scattering in the aftermath of some mighty cosmic explosion. And at the outskirts of the universe, more than seven billion light-years away, scientists have recently identified a number of quasars—vast quasi-stellar entities, many times brighter than all the stars in the Milky Way put together—rushing still farther out and leaving new galaxies to form in their path.

Is there life on Mars? Is Jupiter inhabitable? Is Uranus anything like the earth? We may soon have an answer. But the answer will say very little about the rest of the universe. We are still exploring our closest neighbors in our own solar system. Out there are billions of solar systems, young and old; trillions of planets, large and small. We must remember also that we are looking at the universe from within a very limited time frame, from the perspective of this particular moment in the history of man. Here on earth, our own lifetime is just a fraction of duration compared with the three to four million years of human existence on earth and nothing at all compared with the four to five billion years since the formation of the earth itself. The universe, astronomers now estimate, is probably some fifteen to twenty billion years old, and yet its formation is apparently still not completed.

What can Christians say in the light of such mind-boggling perspectives? What can theologians do with a faith that has emerged only on this relatively insignificant planet, and only within the last two thousand years? Can Christianity in any way be made to encompass the vast universal realities which we are now, slowly, becoming aware of?

I shall not, of course, be able to develop the answer to these questions here—both the mind and the moment are too limited for that. But I would be less than responsible if I did not try to indicate how the Christian faith might relate to the new challenges of today.

As we have seen, the essence of the Christian faith has to do with Christology. Christianity historically has centered on the affirmation that God, the only God, the God of the universe and the Sovereign Lord of creation, at one point in time manifested himself in history, in a certain place and in one particular person, namely, Jesus of Nazareth, who as Christ and Messiah fulfilled the work of universal redemption, once and for all, and thus became the Savior of all mankind. The early church was quite unapologetic about this Christocentricity of faith; one of the earliest known Christian confessions said simply, "Jesus Christ is Lord."

And yet, early Christians soon recognized that in focusing so uniquely on the person and ministry of Jesus, they were in danger of limiting the redemptive work to the impact of one individual, to one historical period, and to a rather limited geographic area. What of the people who lived before Jesus, and what of the generations who were not yet born when he died? What of those in other places, for whom Bethlehem and Nazareth, and even Jerusalem, were totally unknown?

The church developed its answers in several ways. In relation to those who were already dead by the time Christ appeared, the church explained that after he died, Christ went down into the realm of the shadows—Hades, the home of the dead—and there preached his saving word to the spirits of former generations. That is what the curious phrase in the Apostles' Creed, "descended into hell," stands for—and that is why we should keep it in our creed. If we remove that phrase, we leave ourselves without the Christian answer to the question concerning the salvation of earlier generations.

On the other hand, in relation to those who were not yet alive when Jesus died—the generations that were yet to come—the church was soon convinced that although the historical manifestation of the Christ had come to an end—with his death, or after the resurrection, with his ascension—the Holy Spirit was given as a sort of supra-historical continuation of his saving and sanctifying Presence which was not limited to a certain time and place, but universally dispersed and freely accessible to all.

The early church thus answered the questions related to the limitations of time and place by enlarging its Christology in such a way as to tie the historical Jesus—the events enclosed in the parenthesis of his life from cradle to cross—into the universal history of God's dealings with the world, from creation to consummation. It enlarged the message of this Jewish Messiah—first interpreted in terms of traditions contained in the scriptural canon of the people of Israel—so as to make it applicable to all men, whether Jew or Gentile, whether contemporary, preceding, or subsequent in time.

Out of the thelogical reflections which went on in the early Christian church emerged what we have subsequently come to describe as the doctrine of the Trinity—a very difficult concept to understand, but one which says a number of important things about the way early Christians conceived of God and the way they conceptualized his relationship to the world. It says: (1) that God is one; (2) that God manifests himself in a threefold manner in relation to the world: as Father he is the source of all things, maker and ruler of the universe; as Christ he is the redeemer of all men, sharing our history and bearing our burdens; and as Spirit he is the universal presence, the sustainer of life, the comforter and guide, everywhere and at all times.

Armed with this trinitarian theology, the church has so far been able to cope with the various revolutionary developments that have affected man's worldview in the past. The Copernician discovery of the heliocentric universe, for example, at first suppressed by the church for fear that it threatened certain basic biblical truths, was later absorbed into Christian thought. This absorption was accomplished simply by emphasizing that God, the Creator, did a much grander thing than was first understood; he is the creator of the heavens as well as the earth. Even though the earth can no longer be seen as the center of creation, faith can take the whole universe as God's creation and affirm that the earth has its intended or designated place within it.

Similarly, the church learned how to handle the Darwinian discovery of man's place in the evolutionary process. Christians at first discounted the theory for fear that it invalidated the biblical story of creation. After further thought they found they could consider the evolutionary process as part of God's creative work—perhaps even as the method by which the Creator proceeded or a sign that he continues to be active in the world.

These developments are part of the history of theology and are instructive, to a degree. But the question now facing the Christian community is infinitely more complex than any that confronted the early church, the late medieval theologians, or our nineteenth-century predecessors. The new cosmology which astronomers and space scientists are now developing openly challenges the traditional trinitarian conception of God—and on the level of its presuppositions. Our knowledge of the universe points to the relativity of historical

Christian faith more clearly than we have ever been confronted with it before.

The issue before us is this: Can God, the God of the universe, still be thought of in terms of a perspective that puts the planet Earth, or man, in any way at the center of things, whether in the context of creation or in the context of redemption or fulfillment? Can Christ, God incarnate in history, still be thought of in terms of perspectives that take our earthly, human history—and Jesus of Nazareth within it—in any sense as the single, exclusive context for the incarnational dimension of theology? Can the Holy Spirit, God continually present and active in the world, still be thought of in terms of viewpoints that make the Christian church or Christian believers in any way the singular and unique locus of such spirituality? Should the traditional, earth-oriented, man-oriented, and church-oriented trinitarian conception of God be given up for a more universal view—one that will allow Christian believers to live with their faith in full view of the new insight into the nature of reality which modern science now unveils?

The answer, I think, is clear: Christocentric theological reflection must be updated, and now in relation to the realities of the church's situation in the modern world. What this will mean in practice is difficult to predict. However, we can begin to see already the outlines of a Christian theology for the future.

Let me close this chapter by proposing one such outline. In the next chapter I will discuss specifically the kinds of revisions that are now required in the doctrine of the Trinity. Here I will focus on what needs to take place in regard to the doctrines of God, Christ, and Holy Spirit generally.

First, the doctrine of God will have to be enlarged in such a way that God's creative and redemptive work will not be limited in any way to our world, but related to every world, every solar system, every galaxy, every quasar. His power and his work are not restricted to earthly history, but include the beginnings before the formation of the earth and beginnings yet to take place, even after the sun—the star we depend on—has burned out. His fatherhood is not circumscribed by the span of human existence, but encompasses all of life, all forms of life, at whatever stage, and in whatever place—life already spent and life that is yet to come. His love has not singled out this earth, but is equally full, equally true in relation to every part of creation. Thus, in the perspective of the future, every doctrine of God which is in any way biased by earthly considerations is an obsolete doctrine. Such as god is no more than a provincial idol; he is not the One, Sovereign Lord of the universe. Our God, in the future, shall have to be believed on a big scale.

Second, the doctrine of Christ will also have to be enlarged. The redemptive manifestation of God in our history, in the person and work of Jesus of Nazareth, must be seen, not as the only incarnation of God, but as that particular manifestation which relates to us, to man, to this earth. God, as redeemer, has involved himself in our life, to be sure, but his redemptive love is free to express itself in other places—in relation to all creation, all life, however and wherever it has gone awry. The incarnation of the Christ among us—his presence and teaching, his example and death—is conditioned by our needs, our fallenness, our disobedience, our sin. The manifestation of God's redemptive love elsewhere in creation will likewise be conditioned by the situation which prevails there. Thus in the perspective of the future, every Christology which makes the earthly Jesus the exclusive expression of God's saving grace in the universe is too limited a doctrine. Such a view of salvation, however true for man and earth, is too narrow to fit the Creator-Redeemer of the world. The Christ, in the future, must be thought of on the order of a cosmic principle.

Finally, our understanding of the Holy Spirit must be enlarged, also. The Spirit of God is not, as we have come to think, an exclusive gift to a select company of believers; it is poured out, even as the apostles proclaimed, on all flesh, and it rests, as the early biblical writers expressed it, over all primordial waters. The Spirit of God is loose in the universe—ever present, ever active. It is the fullness of God occupying infinity, penetrating all substance, overflowing the brims of space and surrounding the whole creation. In the future, any doctrine of the Holy Spirit which determines its location or delimits its containment is an erroneous doctrine; such a definition of the Spirit of God is more symbolic of the finitude of the human spirit than of God's eternal, all-pervading presence. The Holy Spirit, in the future, must be perceived with the inclusiveness of universality.

Yes, Christianity can be related to the space age. And it must. Ancient believers used to look up into the skies and say:

> When I look at thy heavens, the work of thy fingers,
> the moon and the stars which thou hast established;
> what is man that thou art mindful of him,
> and the son of man that thou dost care for him?
>
> (Ps. 8:3-4)

Modern believers can look into space, more knowledgeably than their forefathers, and sing the ancient refrain with new and more meaningful overtones:

> O Lord, our Lord,
> how majestic is thy name in all the earth!
>
> Thou whose glory above the heavens is chanted. (Ps. 8:1)

Listen to one such modern believer who sings just such a song:

## Christ in the Universe

With this ambiguous earth
His dealings have been told us. These abide:
The signal to a maid, the humble birth,
The lesson, and the young Man crucified.

But not a star of all
The innumerable host of stars has heard
How He administered this terrestrial ball.
Our race have kept their Lord's entrusted Word.

Of His earth-visiting feet
None knows the secret, cherished, perilous,
The terrible, shamefast, frightened, whispered, sweet,
Heart-shattering secret of His way with us.

109

THE EVOLUTION OF CHRISTOLOGY

No planet knows that this
Our wayside planet, carrying land and wave,
Love and life multiplied, and pain and bliss,
Bears, as chief treasure, one forsaken grave.

Nor, in our little day,
May His devices with the heavens be guessed,
His pilgrimage to thread the Milky Way,
Or His bestowals there be manifest.

But, in the eternities,
Doubtless we shall compare together, hear
A million alien Gospels, in what guise
He trod the Pleiades, the Lyre, the Bear.

O, be prepared, my soul!
To read the inconceivable, to scan
The million forms of God those stars unroll
When, in our turn, we show to them a Man.

—Alice Meynell

## CHAPTER 7

# The Trinity in Space-Age Reformulation

In his new book, *Faith and Freedom: Toward a Theology of Liberation* (Abingdon, 1979), Schubert M. Ogden issues a call for the emancipation of theology from its historical role of "rationalization"—giving reasons for positions already taken—to a new role of "critical reflection," defined as a deliberate, methodical, and reasoned way of determining whether something that appears to be the case really is so. Ogden suggests that this theology-emancipated-from-ideology must be guided by two criteria, "appropriateness" and "understandability": "Theology can judge no position to be adequate that is not at once appropriate to the Christian witness as judged by its apostolic norm, and understandable to human existence as judged in terms of common experience and reason."

It would appear that Ogden's two criteria are basically sound. Theology is faith-reflection. If it is to be Christian faith-reflection, it must be true to the essential character of Christian faith; and if it is to be meaningful to present existence, it must be related to our present understanding of things, our experience and reason.

If Ogden's two criteria are to be followed in our present context, the primary task of Christian theologians, I would suggest, must be to take a new look at the Trinity from the perspective of perceptions that have emerged in the space age.

No argument need be raised as to the centrality of the doctrine of the Trinity in the Christian view of things. Although formulated as doctrine only after the close of the New Testament canon, it is clearly consistent with perspectives that developed among Christians during the formative period of the faith. As we have seen, this faith, which originated in the historical encounter between Jesus of Nazareth and his disciples, quickly assumed the character of Christology and of pneumatology, the conviction being that the Spirit of Christ, which was the Spirit of God, continued to manifest itself following the death of Jesus among those who believed. It was not, perhaps, necessary that this trinitarian faith be expressed in the metaphysical notions of Western philosophy—Tertullian's *tres persona*, *ex unitate substantiae*, Athanasius' *homoousia*, Chalcedon's *three hypostases*, and so on. However, that the Christian faith from its beginning had a distinctly trinitarian orientation or structure is clear and undeniable. What Christians said about Christ inevitably involved God, and what they said about the Spirit necessarily tied in with what they said about God and Christ.

There is no need, on the other hand, to raise any argument about the dawning of the space age—the new framework of perception which we have inherited as a birthright in the twentieth century. We are at the centennial of Albert Einstein's birth, in the decades of moon landings and space probes. This generation has seen vast expansions in the knowledge of the universe, in our epistemology, ontology, and cosmology, that threaten to make obsolete perspectives, interpretations, and established truths that have come down to us from past generations.

Einstein taught us that the Newtonian three-dimensional universe, structured on the stable suppositions of mass, motion, gravity, and the absoluteness of distance and time, does not exist; the actual universe is different. It is a four-dimensional reality, and the fourth dimension, time, is not absolute. Mass is energy. Motion is relative. Gravity is simply a property of space-time. Measurements of time depend on the choice of reference. The only absolute in the universe is the speed of light, yet even light is influenced—bends—under the gravitational character of space-time.

As if this were not enough, contemporary astronomers have expanded our horizons far beyond what was even imaginable a few decades ago. They go beyond our own galaxy, which contains one hundred billion suns or solar systems, to another one hundred billion galaxies in a universe that is still expanding, and to the outskirts of the universe, where new galaxies are apparently being formed in the wake of active quasars and where old stars—weakening pulsars—are apparently dying and being sucked up in "black holes" so dense with gravity that not even light can escape.

Then, by way of interplanetary probes to Mars, and most recently to Jupiter and Saturn, we have finally come to raise the question of the possibility of life elsewhere in our solar system, and in the rest of the universe, in a scientific way. The new vistas are fantastic. With billions of galaxies in the universe, trillions of solar systems, young and old, containing planets of every possible description and at every stage of evolution, chances are that the conditions for life—life as we know it, or life in some other form—not only *do* exist, but that they *have* existed in many places in the past and *will* exist in other places in the future. We do not yet know this for a fact; after all, we are still only investigating our closest neighbors in space—and only from the relative time-frame of the third or fourth millionth year in the history of man, on a planet that is only four to five billion years old. The universe itself, astronomers now estimate, came into being some fifteen to twenty billion years ago. The chances of life elsewhere in the universe are now said to be good.

It is obvious that this new understanding of reality is bound to affect theology, and especially the Christian doctrine of the Trinity. It cannot, I think, be allowed to have the effect of eradicating trinitarian thought altogether—that would spell the end of a distinctly Christian faith, and I would not want to encourage a development of that kind. But Christian theology, shaped as it is in the interplay of trinitarian affirmations, must clearly be reformulated in the light of our present understanding of things, otherwise we shall not be able to make sense of the faith in relation to the realities of experience and reason as these are constituted today.

I should think there would be little disagreement among us on this point. It is when it comes to the how and subsequently to the what of this reconceptualization that our views are likely to differ.

In his book *The Trinity* (Seabury Press, 1970), Karl Rahner has offered contemporary theologians the wise counsel to return to the framework of experiential faith and avoid "the wild and empty conceptual acrobatics" that has characterized trinitarian and christological speculation in earlier ages. Not everyone agrees.

Claude Welch, for example, in his article on "Trinity" in *A Handbook of Christian Theology*, indicates that both the existentialist rethinking of the Trinity, which focuses on a "three-fold viewing of God," and the dramatic-symbolic interpretation, which focuses on "the activity of God as creator, redeemer and sanctifier," are inadequate. Says he: "If Christian faith speaks of a real disclosure or revelation of God, then 'Father, Son and Holy Spirit' must refer not simply to human viewing, but to God Himself, not only to ways in which God is related to the world, but to His 'ways of being God.' "[1]

In Welch's view, the doctrine of the Trinity corresponds to the very being of God—though Welch is not altogether certain how the classical analogy of "person" or "personality" is to be used in this context, whether for "God himself" or for his "ways of being God."

Others among us show more willingness to undertake a serious rethinking of the Trinity and to bear the consequences of such rethinking.

One approach comes to view in "process theology." In their introductory exposition of that perspective, in the volume entitled *Process Theology*, John B. Cobb, Jr., and David Ray Griffin apply their own dynamistic-vitalistic ontology to the Trinity, and immediately find themselves in tension with the language of the traditional dogma. They do not see how one can speak of the three "aspects" of God as "persons" in any consistent logical sense:

When "person" is taken in its modern sense, God is one person. When "person" is taken in its traditional sense, two persons can be distinguished, God as creative love and God as responsive love. But these persons have a transcendent and an immanent aspect, and therefore if we add this distinction to the one between the persons we have a quaternity. If instead we add to the thought of the two persons the unity in which they are held together in the one God, then we have a trinity, but the unity is not another person in the same sense that the other two are persons.[2]

All of which causes these theologians to throw their manuscript sheets in the air and declare:

## THE TRINITY IN SPACE-AGE REFORMULATION

The doctrine of the Trinity is the heart of Christian faith, a source of distortion, and an artificial game that has brought theology into justifiable disrepute. . . . Process theology is not interested in formulating distinctions within God for the sake of conforming with traditional trinitarian notions.[3]

Perhaps the most radical challenge to traditional trinitarian dogmatic in recent years was issued by G. W. H. Lampe, regius professor of divinity at Cambridge University, in his Bampton Lectures for 1976, published under the title *God as Spirit*. Professor Lampe advocates a phenomenalistic-analytical point of view, from which the trinitarian model is seen "less satisfactory for the articulation of our basic Christian experience than the unifying concept of God as spirit."[4] Trinitarian orthodoxy is a development in hypostatic metaphysical terms of a conception of God which was originally purely spiritual. It was as a consequence of the church's displacement from the Hebraic-religious framework of thought into the Greek-speculative context that the original conceptions of "God as Spirit," "Christ as the presence of God," and "the Spirit as the presence of Christ" became hypostatized in terms of separate "substances" or "persons." "The Son of God" now became God the Son, giving rise to a confusing process of *communicatio idiomatum* by which the Jesus of the Gospels was considered substantially one with the preexistent Logos. Likewise, the concept of spirit was reduced in meaning from being "a way of speaking about God in his activity to a name for a third, and something like an extra, divine hypostasis."[5]

This hypostatization, says Lampe, is precisely what caused problems among the early fathers of the church—problems of relating the third hypostasis to the second, and to the first, and problems of distinguishing the relationship between the third person and the first from the relationship between the second and the first. These difficulties, however, were unnecessary. Says Lampe:

The Fathers scarcely paused to consider whether the difficulty might not after all be unreal. They did not ask whether they might have arrived at an impasse, not by insisting that the Holy Spirit is God, but by assuming as an axiom that the Holy Spirit is not simply God—*not* God the Father, God in Jesus Christ,

God in every other mode of his self-revelation to mankind and his contact with the world of creation: in short, that the phrase "the Holy Spirit" is not simply synonymous with "God as Spirit," that is, God as the transcendent and immanent Creator, the mover and inspirer and savior of all that is.[6]

Lampe's own approach is recognizably of the monistic brand, related to theologies of the Sabellian or "dynamic-monarchian" types. Such theologies were of course declared heretical by the early councils, mainly because of the heavy domination of Platonistic-metaphysical speculation during the age of the councils and the creeds—"hypostatic acrobatics" dominated the scene, closed the door on the creative imagination of spirit symbolism, and ruled out the imaginative flexibility of spirit terminology. Lampe now wants to recover that imagination and that flexibility.

Lampe's analyses are very perceptive. However, his own rethinking of the Trinity is only partly directed to the task that is before us, namely, the attempt to come to terms with the new dimension in the understanding of reality. What is needed now is a reconceptualization of the Trinity that takes into account the larger spectrum of the modern understanding of things—the cosmic scene, space and time, nature and history, in short, the universe as we know it.

One attempt to do that is Thomas F. Torrance's little book, *Space, Time and Incarnation*. Aimed at examining in a scientific way "the place of spatial and temporal ingredients in basic theological concepts and statements and to clarify the epistemological questions they involve,"[7] the effort is praiseworthy. But there are problems as well.

Torrance recalls the principal conceptions of time and space that have arisen in the history of Western thought—the Aristotelian "finite receptacle," the Pythagorean-Newtonian "infinite receptacle," the Platonic-relational, and the Einsteinian-relativistic ideas—and says: "Now that the receptacle notion of space and time has broken down, we need to rethink the essential basis of Christian theology in the relation of the Incarnation to space-time, and to think completely away the damaging effects of a deistic relation between God and the universe."[8]

So far so good. Torrance then proceeds to combine the Incarnation with the doctrine of creation and to consider space and time the creations of a God who is himself transcendent to space and time while yet making space and time "the continuum of relations" which functions as "the immanent order" of existence. The Incarnation thus takes on the character of "a condescension of God to come Himself into the determinations, conditions, and conceptualities of our world."[9]

This "condescension" of God will be differently understood depending on one's concept of space and time. Torrance's own way of making sense of the Incarnation is "to think of *God's relation to the world in terms of an infinite differential*, but think of *the world's relation to God in terms of a created necessity* in which its contingency is not negated."[10]

Basically, the Incarnation is "the chosen path of God's rationality in which He interacts with the world and establishes such a relation between creaturely being and Himself that He will not allow it to slip away from Him into futility or nothingness, but upholds and confirms it as that which He has made and come to redeem."[11]

However, we are made aware throughout that Torrance operates within a singular and exclusive Creation-Incarnation axis. He says: "Now that the Incarnation has taken place (namely, in Jesus of Nazareth) we must think of it as the *decisive* action of God in Christ which invalidates all other possibilities and makes all other conceivable roads within space and time to God actually unthinkable."[12]

For Torrance it is simply the determinative point that

in the Incarnation the eternal reality of God has actually intersected with our creaturely reality, overlapping with it in Jesus Christ in a definite span of space-time, and thus *constituting Him the one place where man on earth and in history may really know the Father* because that is the place where God himself has elected to dwell among us.[13]

Jesus Christ is thus the one and only normative "space-time track"; he forms "a moving and creative center for the confluence of world-lines within the plenum of space-time."[14]

We can know the Father only by following the space-time track in truth and life that is Jesus Christ; . . . the relation established between God and man in Jesus Christ constitutes Him as *the place in all space and time* where God meets with man in the actualities of his human existence and man meets with God and knows Him in His own divine Being.[15]

Interesting and well argued as Torrance's view is, its problem, from our standpoint, is the limited—one might say pre-Copernican—view of space and time that it represents, or as we could just as well describe it, the earth-centeredness of his concept of space and the clock-time or earth-history orientation of his concept of time. It suffers from what the astronomer Carl Sagan has dubbed "earth chauvinism." Torrance is *aware* of the four-dimensional universe—he says it can provide a possible "topological language" for the expression of the Incarnation faith; he even suggests that it can be useful in expanding our perspectives from "the preoccupation with the life and work of the person of Christ on earth" to

His whole space-time track in the cosmos, to think of it in quite a different series of connections which would have been inconceivable outside that field, but which now thrust themselves upon us demanding recognition as the inner reality and rationality of the Incarnation.[16]

But Torrance does not follow this line of thought to completion. His own conception of the "space-time track" is not related to the four-dimensional space-time of the Einsteinian universe; he seems stuck within a three-dimensional universe ordered by vertical-horizontal lines, directional ups and downs, metaphysical ins and outs. In Torrance's words, any opening of thought "upward" must be "coordinated downward" with "basic statements arising out of our ordinary experience and empirical knowledge."[17] And this, for Torrance, means that the historical actuality of Jesus Christ remains the singular focal-point of Christology and the sole center of Christian theology as a whole. Says he: "Any construct of Christ that has no rooting in actual history can only be a vehicle of our fantasies."[18]

Having obtained an impression of the kind of frustrations theologians now experience in relation to the classical doctrine of the

Trinity and the kinds of revisions they suggest in order to make Christian theology meaningful in the modern context, we must offer a constructive alternative. We have found other alternatives to fall short, primarily because they do not take full account of the new understanding of things, the cosmic scene, space and time, reality as we know it, the universe as it is now understood; but we have found helpful notions and suggestive perspectives as well. It remains for us to attempt to take the rethinking of the Trinity one step farther, toward a sensible correlation with that modern view of things which is at once our generation's highest intellectual accomplishment and, especially for us as theologians, its most serious challenge.

As I see it, the premise of any reflective reconceptualization of trinitarian theology in the present situation must be liberation from the traditional metaphysical approach—what Rahner calls "wild and empty conceptual acrobatics"—and commitment to the religious or spiritual core of trinitarian thought—what Rahner calls "the framework of experiential faith." As is apparent to everyone concerned, the traditional idea of God as a single "substance" with three "hypostases" or "persons" joined together by way of Chalcedonian-type paradoxes—"distinct but not separate, united but not mingled"—will not work any more. It is not even useful as a starting point. To apply such massive concepts to God is bound to cause suspicion in our time, logically as well as theologically. It creates difficulties of a conceptual sort as well.

*Logically* it is clear that as modern men we can speak meaningfully of "substance" only if the "substance" we talk about is understood substantially—i.e., in terms of a substantiality that we are capable of understanding. But to say this is to create difficulties for theology. To suggest that the divine substance is in any way within our conceptual grasp is a prima facie violation of the *theological* injunction against image-making and idolatry. If in order to guard ourselves from this sort of theological reductionism we decide to introduce the concept of "transcendence" and describe God's substantiality as transcendent of everything we can ever grasp or define, then we may be able to satisfy the requirements of *theology*—the emphasis on the absolute otherness of God. But the requirements of *logic and reason* are violated; in fact we are trying to talk about something which we have no understanding of or conceptualize something which by definition is beyond human conceptualization. If, in trying to avoid such obvious *logical* fallacies, we adopt the critical notion that human concepts and language are applied to God only by way of analogy, symbolically, we may find ourselves out of the woods *logically and theologically*, but faced with certain *conceptual* difficulties peculiar to the modern situation. Our understanding of such concepts as "substance" and "person" has changed so radically in the modern age as to force us to undertake a complete reexamination of what these kinds of analogies or symbols actually express. And with that we are tossed right back into the theological crucible, where basic questions must be raised concerning the adequacy of our language about God.

It is of course possible that a reconceptualization of trinitarian theology can be attempted in terms of distinctly contemporary analogies drawn from modern physics and modern personality theory. Instead of the massive view of God, one could operate with a dynamic or quantum view, and instead of the individualistic understanding of personality, one could utilize the social or relational understanding of personhood. People who understand such new ideas can serve us well by reinterpreting classical analogies and symbols along these lines, thus updating the correlation between theological reflection and the modern understanding of things. We may find a solution to some of the problems inherent in classical trinitarian language that way. However, if the intention behind the enterprise is to push the analogies beyond their meaning as metaphors and to press them into service as another form of metaphysical ontology, the final outcome may be nothing more than an exchange of one kind of metaphysics, already suspect from a logical and theological point of view, for another.

It is to avoid such unhappy implications that I declared myself willing to accept Rahner's suggestion that the rethinking of the Trinity must focus on the religious or spiritual core of trinitarian thought—which is nothing else than experiential Christian faith. However, Rahner's suggestion must itself be taken one step farther, namely, toward an analytical *phenomenology* of religious experience.

## THE TRINITY IN SPACE-AGE REFORMULATION

Theology does not construct a new ontology on the basis of human spirituality; spirituality already has one. Its ontology is of empirical nature, not speculative. Theology does not produce "theontology"; what it does is better described—to use Feuerbach's term—as "ontotheology." The ontological basis for theology is simply man's religious experience of the world—expressed theologically as man's "experience of God" in the world. It is in the analysis of the dynamics of spiritual experience—i.e., in the phenomenology of spirit—that theology, Christian theology or trinitarian theological reflection, must be ontologically rooted.

If this phenomenological or ontotheological viewpoint is accepted as a premise, we can move to the assertion that the phenomenology of spirit that forms the ontological basis of Christian theology historically is a threefold one—i.e., the Christian experience of God consists of a threefold or trinitarian dynamic. In classical terminology, it is the experience of God the Father, God the Son, and God the Holy Spirit. From the perspective of the phenomenology of spirit, it is in essence the experience of God as spirit, but in terms of three distinct modes of spirituality—the Creator Spirit, the Incarnate Spirit, and the Indwelling Spirit. Christian spirituality is thus seen to be formed with reference to three distinct dimensions of divine inspiration or three dimensions in the Christian believer's awareness of God.

It should be recognized at this point that from the ontotheological point of view spiritual experience is not so much the experience of spiritual things as it is the spiritual experience of things. *Ontologically*, what the Christian believer experiences is the world, the message of Jesus of Nazareth, and the enlightenment of the self; *theologically*, the Christian interprets these experiences from the standpoint of faith in God who as Spirit is active in the world. Thus the world takes on the character of "creation"; Jesus becomes "Christ"; and the self is renewed by the "indwelling of the Holy Spirit."

As will be recognized, this approach to trinitarian theology is inspired by Professor Lampe's view of God as Spirit. It takes as its leading idea a concept of God that is unified, yet capable of experiential pluralization, and resistant to metaphysical hypostatization. This way we have asserted the possibility of trinitarian

121

theological explication without necessarily being led into logical and theological—i.e., metaphysical and ontological—difficulties. To understand the concept of spirit it is necessary to analyze actual human spirituality—the forms of inspiration or the dimensions of awareness of God that man actually experiences. To understand the character of Christian trinitarian reflection, it is necessary to observe the threefold phenomenology of Christian spiritual experience. It is by way of ontotheological projection that the three dimensions of Christian spiritual experience are considered correspondent to the basic modes of divine self-expression—to the dynamics of divine self-revelation in the world. The first dimension is that which corresponds to God's activity *universally;* the second has to do with God's activity *in particular incarnate form;* and the third has to do with the activity of God *within the life of individual believers.*

If this can be accepted as an adequate ontotheological outline of Christian trinitarian experience and reflection, we can put aside for the moment the task of reinterpreting the classical trinitarian formulas along these lines. I am convinced that it can be done; it is in fact already being done by such scholars as Lampe and Rahner and to a certain extent by Cobb and Griffin. What we are interested in here is the more advanced task of restructuring trinitarian theologizing in the light of realities as we experience them in the space age. Obviously, the new understanding of the universe emerging in our time will have serious implications for the way Christians interpret the activity of God in the world, in Christ, and within the self.

Speaking first of *the activity of God in the world,* it is clear that our vastly expanded awareness of time and space will *force us to reconsider that activity on a vastly larger scale than before.* The universe, we now know, is not an earth-centered one, not even a heliocentric one, not even a galacticocentric one. If it is centric at all, it seems organized around a dynamic vacuum where, some fifteen to twenty billion earth-years ago, i.e., long before the Earth was formed, all the energy which is the *ontos* of all there is in the universe came together—perhaps by the dynamics of some secret cosmic cyclus—exploding in that biggest of all bangs, the beginnings of the present universe, and causing its energy-content to be scattered in a hundred billion galaxies swirling through space, always in motion, relatively and absolutely, and always rushing outward, away from their place of birth.

In light of such vistas, if God is now in any sense to be believed as "the Creator of the universe," the divine Spirit must be seen as active throughout the universe, in every world, every solar system, every galaxy, every quasar; in every beginning and every end; in whatever it was that preceded the big bang and in all that is now going on in the dense black holes where spent energy seems to reassemble as in preparation for other gigantic explosions; in the old regions of the universe as well as in the newer regions, billions of light-years away, where energy is still being transformed to mass. Moreover, if God is to be seen as eternal, it is necessary that we see this concept in relation to the new understanding of time. It is quite trivial and meaningless, for example, to speak of God's eternity simply as an extension of the chronological time-line, with its beginning and end, before and after. Time, we now know, is not absolute; it is a function of perspective, and the perspective of the Earth—now more than ever—is altogether too limited. Ours is a comparatively young solar system located somewhat in the periphery of our galaxy, and therefore a relative newcomer in the heavens. The history of this Earth does not parallel the history of other planets, in other solar systems or in other galaxies. Relative to other planets Earth is both younger and older, less developed and farther advanced. There was a time when Earth did not exist, and there will be a time when it no longer exists. The existence of the Earth does not serve as indicator of beginnings or ends in any universal or absolute sense. Our beginnings may well have coincided with many other ends, and our end may yet be coincidental to other beginnings. The new understanding of time, with its bold assertion of relativity, makes it possible, in fact, to see time as the relativity of eternity itself—as the dynamic pulse of an ongoing universe. The new ontology of time that has developed in the space age can thus help us develop a more meaningful theology of eternity.

The dramatic expansion of our conception of God's activity in the universe needs to be matched by an *equally radical expansion of our reflection on God's activity in Christ*. The redemptive activity of God must be seen to match the universality and eternity of his spirit, and be related to all possible worlds, wherever and whenever there is anything that has gone awry. But this is clearly a problematic idea. The difficulty Christians have to cope with is the fact that we have been conditioned to think of Christ in terms of a singular incarnation— Jesus Christ—and of redemption as a work that is accomplished, once and for all, exclusively in him. In the space age, this is a singularly unsatisfactory thought.

It was always difficult for Christians to defend the particularity and exclusiveness of the incarnation doctrine, yet the point has always been considered synonymous with Christian faith. That God has chosen to make manifest his presence as Savior in a man, in this particular man Jesus and nowhere else, is at once the most emphatic and the most offensive feature in historical Christian doctrine. It puts Christians in the situation of having to deny that the Spirit of God can incarnate itself in any other or additional form and at the same time claiming for themselves the privilege of proclaiming the only saving Word for the world. Such a view—however possible it may have seemed to earlier generations—is clearly no longer possible. In the space age it does not make sense to claim that the earthly incarnation of the divine spirit in Jesus Christ is the only manifestation of the redemptive activity of God in the universe. It is equally nonsensical to think that if salvation is to be effected elsewhere in the universe it must be by way of the earth, by the preaching of Jesus Christ by earthly missionaries. Obviously, contemporary Christians *must* find a way to relate the incarnational dimension of their faith to the cosmic realities as they are.

The way to meet this challenge and to accomplish the christological expansion necessary in the space age, I would suggest, is to relativize the *event* of the incarnation in Jesus and to absolutize the *principle* of the incarnation of God as Christ. From this perspective the redemptive manifestation of God in *our* history, in the person and work of Jesus of Nazareth, is seen, *not as the singular instance of the principle of incarnation, but as one instance of the singular principle of incarnation.* It is the particular instance of incarnation which relates to earth, to man, to us; but it is not the only instance of incarnation, universally. The divine Spirit remains free to involve itself incarnationally, in the interest of redemption, elsewhere and in other forms.

It is difficult, perhaps, for Christians to accept this relativization of the incarnation event; Jesus Christ has so far been the only Christ we recognize. We have particularized Christ, absolutized his particularity, and refused to distinguish between event and principle. Now we are called upon to universalize Christ, relativize his particularity, and consider the Christ-principle capable of self-realization in a plurality of Christ-events. This changes Christology dramatically. Incarnation becomes a dynamic quality of divine Spirit, not a singular event in history. This does not mean that we *deny* the incarnation in Jesus Christ; it simply means that in affirming it we do *not* deny the universal validity of the principle involved. On the contrary, we affirm the Christ-dimension of the divine Spirit—the incarnational dynamic—as an absolute universal principle.

This rethinking of the second aspect of trinitarian theology, God's activity in Christ, leads finally *to a corresponding reexamination of the third dimension of Christian experience and faith, the activity of God's Spirit within.* Once more we are faced with significant expansions of our understanding—space-age perspectives that will both broaden and deepen our perception of spiritual life—whether we view human spirituality as the descent of the divine Spirit upon man, inspiration, or as the evolution of the human spirit toward God, spiritualization. In view of what we have already said about the activity of God as spirit, in the world at large and incarnationally as Christ, the idea that the individual human spirit is in any way directly related to the divine Spirit is simply mind-boggling.

Consider inspiration, for example. It used to be understood simply as a gift of God, a second blessing, a charisma of a special sort. It was spoken of as "the gift of the Holy Spirit," "baptism in the Holy Spirit," or "the fullness of the Holy Spirit." Under the impact of the classical trinitarian tripartitioning of the deity, this experience was thought to relate to one of the hypostases of God, the Holy Spirit, not to essential deity itself. In the light of our present interpretation of God as spirit, on the other hand, all God's activity is the activity of spirit, and all divine inspiration is the activity of God. Inspiration thus takes on entirely new dimensions. The Spirit within is not a fragment or a part, but the essence and fullness of God—the eternal Spirit in the universe condescending to the level of the human spirit, indwelling man and making individual human beings the temples of God. Inspiration, from this perspective, actually becomes something of a correlative to incarnation—which is a highly suggestive idea, both from the standpoint of the dynamics of spirituality and from the standpoint of Christology.

Then consider spiritualization. It has often been understood simply as the development of human spirituality, the fulfillment of man's potentialities as man, the ennoblement of the human spirit. Under the old view of spirituality, such "synergism" was regularly condemned as constituting spiritual presumption and self-salvation; there was an absolute chasm fixed between human spirituality—humanism—and God's Spirit. Within our present understanding of God as spirit, on the other hand, all spirituality is essentially related to the activity of God and all activity of God related to human spirituality. Spiritualization thus comes to represent, not man's isolated efforts to ennoble himself, but evidence of the continuing activity of God in whose image and likeness man was made a living spirit to begin with and under whose tutelage he grows to maturity in spirit. From this perspective, spiritualization actually takes on some of the implications of the classical doctrine of deification—once more an idea that is highly suggestive, both from the standpoint of Christology and from the standpoint of the dynamics of spirituality.

If, in summary, I should attempt to capsule what I think Christian trinitarian theological reflection would look like when approached from the perspectives of the space age, I would propose the following formula as a working hypothesis: (1) that the contemporary Christian view God as the divine Spirit active in the universe—i.e., as the creative force at work universally, as the redemptive presence incarnate where there is need, and as the indwelling spirit wherever there is spirituality; (2) that the symbol of this new Trinity not be the triangle, but a sphere, coterminous with the universe and penetrated by a dynamic dimension which energizes the whole, actualizes itself in the particular, and inspires everything and everyone who is possessed of spirituality; and (3) that to relate this view to classical trinitarian thought, one can simply say that "God the Father" is here the universal divine Spirit; "God the Son" or "Christ" the historical actualization—incarnation—of divine Spirit; and "God the Holy Spirit" the personal interiorization—indwelling—of divine Spirit.

# NOTES

Hall, Thor, 1927-
The evolution of Christology

Chapter 3

1. Much of the material in this chapter is from my article "Let Religion Be Religious," in *Interpretation*, vol. 23, 1969. Used by permission.
2. Thor Hall, *Advent-Christmas*—Series B (Proclamation I). Copyright 1975. Used by permission of Fortress Press.
3. Hall, "A New Syntax for Religious Language," in *Theology Today*, vol. 24, 1967. Used by permission.

Chapter 5

1. Hans Küng, *On Being a Christian*, trans. by Edward Quinn (Garden City: Doubleday & Company, 1976), pp. 153-54.
2. *Ibid.*, pp. 98-99.
3. For further discussion of the issues involved in the relationship of Christianity and the world religions, cf. my article, "Nygren's Approach to Methodological Issues in Interfaith Dialogue," *Religion in Life*, vol. 47, 1978, pp. 171-89.

Chapter 7

1. Claude Welch, *A Handbook of Christian Theology* (New York: New American Library, 1959).
2. John B. Cobb, Jr., and David Ray Griffin, *Process Theology* (Philadelphia: The Westminster Press, 1976), p. 109.
3. *Ibid.*, p. 110.
4. G. W. H. Lampe, *God as Spirit* (New York: Oxford University Press, 1977), p. 228.
5. *Ibid.*, p. 135.
6. *Ibid.*, p. 222-23.
7. Thomas F. Torrance, *Space, Time and Incarnation* (New York: Oxford University Press, 2nd ed., 1978), p. v.
8. *Ibid.*, p. 59.
9. *Ibid.*, p. 61.
10. *Ibid.*, p. 66 (emphases mine).
11. *Ibid.*, p. 67.
12. *Ibid.*, p. 68.
13. *Ibid.*, p. 76.
14. *Ibid.*, p. 72.
15. *Ibid.*, p. 75.
16. *Ibid.*, p. 85.
17. *Ibid.*, p. 89.
18. *Ibid.*, p. 90.